LOCAL GOVERNMENT

■ How to get into it

■ How to administer it effectively

LOCAL

Byron S. Matthews

GOVERNMENT

■ How to get into it

■ How to administer it effectively

NELSON-HALL COMPANY, Chicago

Standard Book Number 911012-04-4

Library of Congress Catalog No.78-110451
*Nelson-Hall Co., Publishers, 325 W. Jackson Blvd.
Chicago, Illinois 60606*

Manufactured in the United States of America

*This book is dedicated,
with respect and admiration,
to the half-million overworked,
unappreciated and dedicated
local government officials
in the United States.*

Contents

Preface

On local government rests the responsibility for providing essential services which make possible our way of life. It provides and administers traffic regulation, crime prevention, fire protection, sewage disposal, garbage removal, water filtration, parks, schools and libraries.

An effective local government is one that is directed by competent officials, staffed with dedicated employees, and backed by enlightened citizens.

It is important, too, that officials and the public know how local government functions, and what methods are most effective for getting things done. The purpose of this volume is to provide such edification.

A working handbook of good government, it was written for elected and appointed officials, for those who aspire to public office, for members of various administrative boards, for PTA and other civic groups, and for all concerned citizens.

Acknowledgments

It would be difficult to name all the people who helped me with this book. Almost every public official who has talked to me in the past gave me ideas. Many interested citizens who never held public office offered suggestions. Much of the information was stored in my memory before I even thought of writing.

Alfred Aaronson, the dedicated leader of the Tulsa City-County Library Board, made his personal records available and gave me valuable background information on how to win a referendum. I was inspired, too, by Otto Kerner, a former governor of Illinois and later a federal judge, who emphasized the importance of local governments in his decisions as a Cook County jurist many years ago.

And finally, city officials in Illinois, from Arlington Heights to Zion, have contributed to these pages through their practical demonstration of the methods that result in effective local government.

1
What is local government?

THERE ARE OVER FIFTY thousand local governments of all kinds in the fifty states. These are governed by hundreds of thousands of elected or appointed trustees, aldermen or commissioners. Together they affect practically all phases of every person's daily life, the value of his property, his health, and even his dreams for the future.

Local government planning is an important field that the public rarely notices even when it is done right. People in Tulsa, Oklahoma, take their water for granted, without stopping to think about the city officials of 1922 who planned far enough ahead to put in a gravity tunnel to bring water 54 miles to the city. There was plenty of water while Tulsa grew from 72,000 in 1922 to 262,000 in 1960. Many cities have looked far ahead like this; but we hear more often about cities like New York, where daily problems have kept officials from looking far enough ahead to avoid water shortages.

Local governments led the nation in protecting the public from air pollution. In recent years, the United States government and a few proposed regional agencies have been getting attention for proposals to fight air pollution. Some local governments have been using their weapons to fight air pollution for more than three-quarters of a century.

Chicago passes 1881 ordinance

Chicago passed a smoke ordinance, with a penalty for violation, in 1881. More recently, during the last thirty years, local governments have moved to reduce air pollution, mostly by regulating smoke from industries. When local officials become alerted to this kind of problem, they are not bogged down by the resistances that larger governments have; they can move effectively and promptly. They can get studies made by competent engineers, have their attorneys prepare an ordinance, and put a program into effect within weeks of the time that they recognize the problem.

Good schools go a long way toward helping men realize their dreams for their future and that of their children. Most public grade, junior high and high schools are run by local school boards. In many cities, the local school board is independently elected, and responsible directly to the local voters. Effective school boards must do more than get the cooperation of school administrators and the teachers. They must also have the support of the public. Where public support is lacking, the schools can't pass bond issue elections, and can't pass tax increase elections. This will directly affect property values in the district; where school activities have to be curtailed, values of homes are lower.

Law enforcement is a complex job for local government today. Court decisions seem designed to make it easy for the accused to escape conviction. Disorderly behavior sometimes gets out of control. Crime is on the increase. Yet, in some cities, local government has reduced crime. These are cities where the people know they can complain effectively about oppression by a policeman, therefore the police are not viewed as enemies.

A few years ago, some political scientists were predicting the decline of the cities. Now, most long-range predictions consider that urbanization is growing and will create problems that can, and must be, solved locally. We will have local government because we need it. We can have more effective local government if we plan for it.

To plan for local government, we must first understand it.

Advantages and disadvantages

All local governments are not the same. There are three principal kinds of local governments. The first includes cities, villages and towns: these are called municipalities.

The second kind covers districts formed to meet one particular need: school districts, park districts, fire protection districts, public water supply districts and sanitary districts. These are sometimes called ad hoc districts or special districts. The latest example is a transportation authority or transit authority, created to solve commuter train and bus problems in a metropolitan area.

The third type is the county government. A county government has many powers and duties that overlap other local governments' work. In practice, local officials usually manage to work together by dividing authority.

Figures 1 and 2 outline the kinds of local governments.

State laws and local practices vary; you will be able to understand your own government better if you understand the most common varieties of local government and their advantages and disadvantages.

City governments have several forms. The oldest is the

mayor and alderman form of city government. The mayor is elected by the entire city, and the aldermen are elected by wards. In some cities there are two aldermen from each ward. A few larger cities have only one alderman from each ward. The aldermen and mayor meeting together are the city council. The mayor acts as chairman; the city council passes local laws, called ordinances, and controls spending.

Fig. 1
FORMS OF LOCAL GOVERNMENT

Name	Governing Body	Characteristics
City	Mayor and Aldermen (City Council)	Complete local government. Strong Mayor.
Commission Form City	Mayor and Commissioners (City Commission)	Complete local government. No one strong man.
Manager Plan City	Mayor and Aldermen (or Mayor and Commissioners) and Manager.	Complete local government. Manager has broad powers.
Village	President and Trustees (Village Board)	Complete local government. Strong President.
Home Rule City or Special Charter City	Mayor and Commissioners or Mayor and Aldermen.	Complete local government. Flexible form.
Incorporated Town	President and Trustees (Town Board)	Complete local government. Similar to a village.
Township	Township Board, and all voters at the Town Meeting.	Road construction. Public welfare.
Metropolitan Government	Elected governing board.	Complete local government, covering one or more entire counties.
County	County Commissioners or County Supervisors. (County Board)	Roads, sheriff, courts, public welfare, building and zoning, health department work.

Special districts: School District, Fire Protection District, Airport Authority, Drainage District, Library District, Park District, Sanitary District, Transportation Authority, Water Supply District. See Figure 2.

Where there are two aldermen from each ward, usually they serve four-year, staggered terms. That is, one alderman from each ward comes up for election every two years.

As the local legislative body, the city council has the same duties locally that the state legislature has on a state level. There are many kinds of regulations that can best be handled locally: traffic regulation, curfew, rules for the police department, and zoning, for example.

The city council is the equivalent of big business when it handles the public's money. It levies its share of local taxes, provides a budget or appropriation ordinance, and decides when to have a bond issue. Many kinds of bond issues cannot be passed without a referendum, but the city council decides in the first place whether to have a referendum. The city council also calls for bids for all major purchases and contracts.

Division of responsibility

In a city that has a mayor and aldermen, the responsibility for running the city is divided between the mayor and the aldermen. If a strong mayor runs a city almost single-handedly, he does it by controlling the aldermen. The aldermen always have some work to do and some decisions to make.

Aldermen can use the committee system to advantage. In a large city where there is no time for the entire council to listen to each citizen on a particular problem, committee hearings can let everybody talk. The committee, after considering what the individuals have to say, then reports to the entire council.

Organization by wards gives each citizen in a large city one man that he can look to as his own representative. There is an orderly way for him to be heard by the city government. He can talk to the alderman from his ward. He also can go to the committee that has charge of his problem.

In practice, this system also has proven to have disadvantages in some instances; every system has some. First, there is the possibility that a strong political machine will build up. Where the only way to get anything done by the city is through the alderman, the next step is to make it a practice that the way to get to see the alderman is to apply to a precinct captain. In its worst form, little gets done without the help of the political machine.

A qualified advantage, in a mayor-aldermen city, is that government in each ward is responsive to the will of the people in that ward. This means that even though organized crime and vice may be tolerated in parts of a large city, citizens can organize to have clean government in their particular ward by electing an honest alderman. Everyone familiar with politics knows of examples of honest wards, and wards where vice is tolerated, in the same city.

Another form of city government, the commission form city, is the exact opposite of the mayor-alderman form. This system became popular in the first half of the twentieth century, and was widely adopted as more efficient than the mayor-alderman form. The duties of running the city are sharply divided among the commissioners. Usually there are five commissioners. The mayor is one of the commissioners, with not much more actual authority than any of the other four. As in any other city, though, the title of mayor gives the man a chance to wield more influence in practice than he has on paper. A strong man can do a lot, if the other commissioners let him do it.

Assigning responsibility

While forms vary from state to state, there is a definite part of the government assigned to each commissioner in every commission form city. The commissioner of accounts and finances has to watch the budget and appropriations, and make sure no unauthorized spending goes on. This means he must work out compromises among the other commissioners, since there never is enough money. The commissioner of public safety heads up the police and fire departments; the chief of police reports to him.

The street commissioner must keep up with all the latest techniques of road design and construction. Chapter 5 shows how broad his possibilities are. The commissioner of public property must keep up not only with existing buildings, but also know what each of the other commissioners thinks is needed for future planning.

The mayor is the commissioner of public affairs, and is really only one of the commissioners. He has no veto power, not much appointing power, and hence none of the weapons that a mayor of a mayor-alderman city can use to exert influence. How much he manages to lead depends on what he can put into the job in the way of persuasiveness and leadership.

The commissioners not only run their own separate departments, but also act as the governing body of the city. The commissioners, including the mayor, meet as the city commission, to do the same things that the city council does in a mayor-aldermen form city. This means that the commissioners are both legislators and executives: legislators when they meet as the city commission, and executives the rest of the time when they are running their departments.

Recognition of leaders

The commission form has the advantage of letting the voters know all of their city commissioners, as there are only five men. It permits the voters or slatemakers to select a few qualified men from the entire city. There is a disadvantage at times in trying to get unity: the city may seem to have five mayors.

The most popular form of government right now is the manager plan. Many cities have switched to the manager plan in recent years. Its strongest proponents call it the solution to all the city's problems. Actually, the manager plan is simply a way to organize the administrative arm of the city.

Although there are several variations of the manager form of government, they all have one thing in common: the manager is the appointed executive head of all departments. In extreme cases this could reduce the mayor to a ceremonial figurehead like a constitutional monarch. In practice, the mayor still has many duties, including presiding at the council meetings and leading the council. The manager is not supposed to set policy; he is the servant of the local legislative body. The city council, city commission, or village board still must pass all legislation, make appropriations, and approve contracts and bills.

In spite of these limitations, managers sometimes are able to do a great deal of decision making. The city council may ask the manager to present information on air pollution. Sometimes the members of the council will take the next step and ask the manager for recommendations. Often the manager has the job of writing the agenda for the meetings. If the manager is not afraid to assume responsibility, he will be able to influence policy.

Village board

A typical form of local government for small-to medium-sized municipalities is a village board. The village board consists of a president and usually six trustees, elected from the entire village. Usually the trustees serve four-year terms, with half the trustees coming up for election every two years.

"Village" refers to the form of government of a municipality, not its size. A village may be ten times the size of a small city.

Election of trustees from the entire village has some advantages: if a majority of the voters in the entire village want honest government, they can vote out a dishonest trustee, even though he may be strongly entrenched in one part of the village. A dishonest alderman could not be removed so easily if he had enough strength in his ward, even though a majority of the city's voters would be glad to see him out.

Election of all officials at large has a disadvantage, though. Parts of the city may have no voice in the local government. In a large village with several distinct districts, one district could furnish all the officials. In practice, village slate makers are careful to pick candidates from all parts of the municipality.

A village can have a manager. Where there is a village manager, he is responsible to the village board just as a city manager is responsible to the city council or city commission. The procedure for appointing a manager varies from one state to the next; in some states, a referendum is required to adopt the manager plan.

Home rule government

There is a kind of municipality that is called a home rule government. Basically, home rule means that the voters of a municipality can, by referendum, adopt a charter and amend the charter for the city. This makes local government much more flexible, in theory. In practice, home rule municipalities usually follow the pattern of one of the types of government outlined in this chapter: mayor-alderman, city commission, village board, or a manager plan.

There is a form of municipality called a town, organized much like a village, with a town board instead of a village board. Do not confuse this with a township, which is a unit of local government with limited powers. A township can build roads, aid the poor, and sometimes provide water, but does not have the general powers that a city, a village, or a town has.

Sharply contrasted with these cities, villages and towns is the second kind of local government: the special districts or ad hoc districts. Each meets just one kind of need. Figure 2 lists the most common kinds.

Probably the most familiar form of special district is the independent school district. Many voters believe that the school district is always an arm of the city government. Often this is not so. Most school districts are completely indepen-dent, answerable only to the voters, levy their own taxes, sell their own bonds, and set their own policies.

School district boundaries do not necessarily coincide with

city or village boundaries. You may know parents who moved to a suburb known for excellent schools, only to find their home was in a different school district entirely. School districts can be side by side and have entirely different problems. One may have plenty of industry for a strong tax base, and the next may have almost no industry, and not enough tax money.

Fig. 2
SPECIAL DISTRICTS

Name	Governing Body	Characteristics
Airport Authority	Board of Trustees (Usually appointed)	Airports and airport zoning (height) rules.
Drainage District	Board of Trustees (Sometimes elected)	Improve streams, dig channels.
Fire Protection District	Board of Fire Trustees.	Fire fighting equipment. (Usually volunteer firemen.)
Library District	Board of Library Trustees (Library Board)	Library services: books, lectures, music.
Park District	Park Board (Usually independently elected.)	Parks and recreation.
Sanitary District	Board of Trustees	Sewage treatment, sewer mains, storm water drains.
School District	Board of Education (Usually independently elected.)	Kindergarten through high school, sometimes through junior college.
Transportation Authority	Board of Trustees	Furnishes and coordinates all kinds of public transportation.

There is now a pilot program providing for local school boards in inner city areas, each controlling just one school. The purpose is to give parents and local residents more voice in the way schools are run. Like any other kind of local government, it will work well in the hands of people with good judgment and will do harm in the hands of people with poor judgment. I am sure that proponents and opponents will be able to find good and bad examples.

There has been a trend in the last twenty years for larger consolidated districts to replace smaller one-room school districts. Good roads and busses make this possible.

School districts have a wide range of duties and activities: Chapter 9, "No One Is Against Better Schools," gives an idea of the scope.

Park district and commissioners

A park district, like a school district, is often an independent local government. The park district is governed by a park board, also called a board of park commissioners. If the park district is independent, the park board is elected; otherwise it is appointed.

The park board does not have to be subservient to the city government to make coordinated effort possible. The park board can work with the city government, as well as with other nearby park districts and other local governments, by voluntary cooperation. Chapter 2, "The Revolution In Park Land Management", suggests some ways.

An independent park district can give consistently good service even during times when the city or village government is in a state of flux. Some park districts have kept the same park board, and the same long range plan, while the village covering about the same area has gone through several extreme changes in government and policy. Long range planning in parks is essential now, and good parks are vital to property values and to the good life.

There is a type of local government, unknown to many people, which can solve a serious problem. In the summer of 1968, a volunteer fire department made news by refusing to put out a fire in a home that had not contributed a fee for the service. This fire department was not a local government organization; it was a private, not-for-profit corporation. While it did not have to put out the fire, it made no friends by watching someone's home burn.

There is a better way: the fire department could form a fire protection district. If the state law does not now provide for a fire protection district, people can ask the state legislature to pass enabling legislation.

A fire protection district is a taxing body with the power to collect taxes, sell bonds, and provide equipment and firemen. The governing body is the board of trustees; in some areas they are elected, and in some states they are appointed by county officials. With a fire protection district, everyone in the district is entitled to the services of the fire fighters. This solves the problem of refusing to put out a fire because someone did not pay the fire department.

Even with a taxing fire protection district, the fire department will probably want to raise extra money. Most fire departments have dances, sales, and parties to raise money for extras. The same thing happens in city fire departments as well.

A fire protection district is usually formed in a rural area, or in a newly incorporated area, that does not have a fire department. The advantage of this district is that it can be formed and give protection in an area that is not part of any city.

Special districts

Water districts, drainage districts, and sanitary districts are other examples of local governments formed to serve just one purpose. A water district, sanitary district, or drainage district may be formed either where there is no city government, or where there are several nearby cities or villages with needs that cut across city boundaries.

Almost all of Cook County, Illinois, including many cities

and villages, is in one sanitary district, the Metropolitan Sanitary District of Greater Chicago. This sanitary district provides a central plant for a large area; thus, many separate cities and villages do not have to provide separate systems.

Portland Cement Association

Fig. 3

An inevitable result of exploding population is the burgeoning growth of suburbs. Thousands of new communities have erupted on prairies and deserts, on ocean fronts and mountain sides. They focus attention on the acute need for honest, efficient local government.

Most sanitary districts, on the other hand, serve only one or two communities. The large district shows how a particular problem can be met on a large scale.

County government is different enough from other kinds of local governments to be in a separate class. County government has powers that cut across almost all of the other kinds of local governments, and provides some services that other local governments do not have.

A county government may, like a city, have a health department, pass health regulations, and require inspections of restaurants and food dealers. A county can provide a county hospital. Usually a county health department will supplement local health departments. In DuPage County, Illinois, the county health department makes agreements with city and village health departments, whereby the county makes health inspections for them. Small cities get the services of a qualified inspector. The county insists that the city health ordinance must be as strict as the county's, if the county is to help by making inspections.

What the county government does

Counties build and maintain roads, provide a courthouse and court system, a jail and rehabilitation services, welfare relief, and in some cases set up building regulations, zoning regulations and other local laws. The sheriff is a county law enforcement officer. County assessors and tax collectors are essential to bringing in revenue needed by all local governments. The county superintendent of schools can be an important coordinator of local effort in education. Chapter 9, "No One Is Against Better Schools," explains how cooperative work by school districts in the same area can help meet increasing demands on limited budgets.

One major difficulty that county governments have is that officials in a big county are isolated from the bulk of the people they represent. This is inevitable in a large population: officials of a county with three million people cannot be as accessible as officials in a village with three thousand. No one would seriously consider breaking up county governments into smaller units because there are area-wide needs that can best be met by county governments.

Often confused with county government are the county-wide

ad hoc districts or special districts. These are specialized local governments whose boundaries may happen to be quite similar to the county boundaries. For example, the Metropolitan Sanitary District of Greater Chicago has the responsibility of providing sewage treatment for nearly all of Cook County. It is not a part of the county government at all, but a separate local government with its own governing body and its own enabling legislation.

There are some ad hoc local governments that cover even more than one county: the Southeastern Pennsylvania Transportation Authority handles commuter traffic over several counties.

A plan of local government that has been suggested more often than it has been tried is metropolitan government, or Metro. A metropolitan government is an agency having all of the powers and duties of the city and county government, but covering a much larger area than a city. Dade County, Florida, is an experiment in metropolitan government, handling all city and county government duties, and even running the airports, in the Miami area. Proponents claim that this is more efficient than smaller local governments.

Metropolitan vs. cooperative government

Actually no one has demonstrated that Dade County, or any similar experiment, has accomplished more than local governments have. Anything that metropolitan government can do single-handedly, smaller local governments can do cooperatively. Throughout this book there are suggestions and specific examples of efficiency gained by cooperation among local governments. For example, a small library can get the same volume discount from publishers that a large library can, by buying cooperatively with other small libraries. Chapter 8, "Libraries Are For People, Not Books," tells how.

Metropolitan government has one built-in flaw: it takes officials further away from the people. Unlike county government, which must cooperate with local governments to get better results, the metropolitan government has no local officials to make it responsive to local sentiment.

While I do not claim to be able to unravel the causes of unrest, one of the reasons must be frustration at having too little voice in government affairs. Creation of metropolitan governments diminishes the voice of the little man in governmental affairs.

Actually, no one form of local government is right or wrong. The people who man the local governments are the ones who must be right, not wrong. If local government is doing a good job in your community, the form you have is workable.

The rest of this book will help you decide whether your local government is efficient.

2

The revolution

in park land management

THE FAST-MOVING EVENTS of the past fifteen years have shown that park land management must always look far ahead. Every few years more park land is needed, less land is available and land costs are higher. To keep up, park land management has been quietly revolutionized.

There are principally two reasons why more land is needed every few years. One is the rapid increase in population, which has more than doubled in many cities and park districts. The second is that almost everyone wants more recreation: people have more leisure time, know they need exercise, and are interested in activities provided by Little League, church leagues and the like.

First, let's look at the kind of growth problems that have

been faced and solved by park districts.

Back in 1952 a midwestern park board bought more land than it needed for the foreseeable future for $1,000 an acre. A few years later, land farther from the center of town could found for $2,000 an acre. The town grew and the vacant areas filled with homes and stores. By 1966, the $1,000 per acre land was worth approximately $10,000 per acre.

The same park board needed still more land in 1966. It used the same system of going to the edge of the town to buy vacant park sites. Since the 1952 purchase had proved the value of foresight, the voters approved a large bond issue for more land in 1966, at the cost of up to $10,000 per acre. If the park board had not bought more than seemed necessary in 1952, it would be behind with no way to catch up.

By contrast, in another park district twenty-five miles away, the park board waited until it was sure it would need the land before acting. By that time the land close enough to the centers of population was not vacant. The park board had to buy apartment buildings and tear them down to get a few small playground sites. It will never have enough park land.

There is no sign that the present trend of rising land costs will end. The Lord is making more people, but He is not making more land. Park boards must look ahead and secure as much land as possible now.

Squeeze on park land

You can see how urgent this will be by studying Figure 1. Notice how fast the population has been growing, especially in cities that looked small a few years ago. The typical land costs have been climbing as rapidly. This puts the squeeze on park land management; there are more people needing more expensive land all the time.

The steady climb in typical prices also emphasizes the need for timely land acquisition. In plain language, the sooner you buy land, the less it will cost.

Fig. 4
EXAMPLES OF CITIES WITH RAPID GROWTH RATES

	1940	1950	1960	1969+
Anaheim, Calif.	11,031	14,556	104,184	160,300
Bellefontaine Neighbors, Mo.	---	---	13,650	23,100
Carpentersville, Ill.	1,289	1,523	17,424	25,800
Hialeah, Fla.	3,958	19,271	66,972	83,800
Jackson, Miss.	62,107	98,271	144,422	171,200
Messapequa Park, N.Y.	488	2,334	19,904	24,600
Shively, Ky.	1,273	2,401	15,155	20,300*
Skokie, Ill.	7,172	14,832	59,364	72,000
Tucson, Ariz.	35,372	45,454	212,892	257,500
Warren, Mich.	582	727	89,246	167,000

Source: U.S. Bureau of the Census.
+Source: Standard Rate and Data Service estimates up to June, 1969
·May, 1967 estimate

Vacant land has a tendency to attract buildings. Land with homes, apartments or industries on it is too expensive for most park districts to buy. This makes it urgent to acquire as much vacant land as possible as soon as possible.

Careful planning of financing of land purchases can stretch tax dollars and make it possible to buy more land for the same long range cost. This is true because of the lower interest rates paid on certain kinds of park bonds. Usually park land is paid for by the sale of bonds, with the interest paid twice a year and the principal due over a period of years.

If the interest rate can be kept down, money will be saved. This results in more dollars to buy land. A one per cent lower interest rate, on a twenty year bond, will save enough in twenty years to buy twenty per cent more land. You don't have to wait twenty years to use the money saved; lower interest payments mean that the same annual taxes can cover higher principal payments. It's like a family being able to meet the house payments more easily when the interest rate is lower.

The park district can keep the interest low by selling general obligation bonds instead of revenue bonds. General obligation bonds are a debt of the park district, to be paid out of tax money. These bonds are the most secure, therefore they pay the lowest interest rate.

Revenue bonds

Revenue bonds, on the other hand, are paid only out of earnings of a particular park facility. Because revenue bonds are not quite so secure, they carry a higher interest cost. Revenue bonds can be helpful in certain situations. If the park district still needs money for more land after it has sold enough general obligation bonds to use up its debt limit set by state law, it will have to issue revenue bonds. Typical revenue bonds are for a swimming pool, stadium or golf course. In some states the law even permits a park board to build an airport with revenue bonds.

Usually a park district must have a referendum before it issues general obligation bonds. The chapter on "How to Pass a Referendum" tells how to insure a good chance to win.

Many park boards have received gifts of land or money, but few realize there is an effective way to attract gifts. In 1945 the Wheeling, West Virginia park system didn't have enough money to maintain the parks it had. Then, in desperation, the park officials established their special trust fund. Anyone could contribute any amount by direct gift or by will. The donor didn't have to be wealthy enough to set up his own trust fund. Without this special fund, only a few people might have remembered to leave a little money to the park fund. With it, many large and small gifts have come in over the years. The total capital in the fund is now $1,200,000.

Watch out for the gift of land with restrictions on its use. If the deed says the land can be used for parks only, the park board will never be able to trade any of it for other property that might in the future be better. Attorneys in a community near Chicago had to struggle to figure out how to trade a little restricted library land for a little restricted park land to improve access to a park. If the giver must impose restrictions, try to have the restrictions expire by their own terms after twenty years.

Beside acquiring as much land as possible, the park boards have learned to make the same land go further. You can use a number of ways to stretch the use of land.

Good lighting can extend the use of land by many hours each day. Lights cost less than land, and can double the amount of use of a baseball diamond or a tennis court.

Strolling areas aren't used as much as they once were after dark, because people fear they'll be the victims of crime. The way to get people back into parks is to make the areas more visible. The shrubs that hide the walk could be replaced by low-lying plants. Painful as it may be to remove shrubs, it is more painful to see parks remain empty. Bright lights complete the job of making the entire area clearly visible.

Another effective way to discourage crime in the parks is to attract people for recreation programs. Chapter 3 explains how to persuade as many people as possible to participate in recreational park activities by introducing every kind of recreation that's feasible.

Year-round use of park land

Plan to use the land the year around. The summer sailing or model boat lagoon can be a winter ice-skating rink. The tennis court can also be an ice-skating rink, if it is flooded right. (A blacktop tennis court will absorb the sun's heat and melt ice quickly, however, unless the court is painted with a white marking material before flooding. The white will reflect the heat, and the ice will stay.)

Flowers, shrubs and trees in the strolling areas can be varied so that there will be attractive, colorful displays from early spring to late fall. The Chicago Park District has discovered that its greenhouses attract visitors every day of the year, even when outdoor gardens are covered with snow and slush.

The exploding need for more park land forced the invention of another forward-looking technique: the park school plan.

The park school plan is a planning device that turns a problem into an asset. The problem is that school facilities are used only until the middle of the afternoon on school days and almost not at all on weekends, holidays and about seventy days of the summer. Similarly, fewer people use the park system when school is in session.

Park-school plan

The solution is to find a school use for the parks during school hours, and a park use for the schools after classes are dismissed. For example, a new school and a new park can be built next to each other. The school will have no separate school playground at all, but it will have outside entrances to the toilets and outside drinking fountains. The park will have enough playground space for school gym and recess needs, but it won't need a building.

Because tax dollars aren't spent for facilities that are idle half the time, the public wins. The park board wins, too, by getting more land for its money, since it saves building costs and does not even need a building site. The school board similarly saves the cost of the ground as well as the upkeep and planting costs.

Geneva, Illinois, has worked out an advanced park school plan. The school board and the park board cooperated to build a combination high school and field house. Part of the structure was paid for by the park district, and part by the school board. A complete agreement for dividend operation and use was worked out before the foundations were poured.

Even though you are not building new schools and parks,

you can use a modified park school plan. There are some parks that are near enough to schools to be used for gym classes. School officials can lease school playgrounds to the park board for use at certain hours. A football practice field can be set up in a park far from the high school since football players are dedicated enough to ride a bus to practice.

The park school plan is not the only kind of cooperative effort being worked out. Some park administrators have discovered that the city public works department or forestry department will lend or rent equipment. In return, the park district can lend or rent tree-trimming equipment, stump-removal machines and sidewalk snowplows to the city. Crews can also be loaned. Money saved by avoiding duplication is money saved for more land.

The chapter on federal aid will help you decide what federal money is available. Your district must decide for itself whether to take it or not.

It is a lucky park district that has not run into the opposite of cooperation from other agencies. There seems to be an unwritten rule in some offices that park land is so unimportant that it can be taken for any other use.

Park board officials in Tulsa discovered that the airport authority's long range plan showed a runway through a public park. No one had thought it necessary to report this to the park board. This situation is not unique: many public officials think that park land is available for any other use. The thousands who use the park are expected to step aside for the hundreds who use the airport.

National and local picture

The answer is to point out everything that this chapter reveals about the needs for more and more park land. Figure 4 showed the national picture. Figure 5 depicts a typical local situation. You can compare this with your district.

With urban population rising, more people living in apartments instead of single family homes, more leisure, and better recognition of the need for regular exercise, parks are not a luxury. Evidence proves that extreme overcrowding can contribute to all the symptoms of social breakdown. No part of the park system should be sacrificed for an allegedly more important use: no other use is more important.

Fig. 5

REPORT ON LAND REQUIREMENTS FOR A TYPICAL PARK DISTRICT

Year	Population	Acres of Parks	Acres per 1000 People	Cost per Acre
20 yrs. ago	5,000	10	2	$ 500
10 yrs. ago	10,000	100	10	$ 2,000
Now	25,000	200	8	$10,000
10 yrs. from now	40,000	400	10	$20,000

Source: Land acquisition files of a park district in a growing suburban area.

In spite of the many imaginative land management ideas that you can get, your park district will probably run out of land five to ten years from now. The two trends of rising population and increased use of the parks make this likely. Decide how much land to buy now, before prices go up more.

You can easily compare the situation in your park district with the typical pattern shown in Figure 5. Most of the figures, including estimates of population expected in future years, are available at the local library, the chamber of commerce and at the city hall. The utility companies and the chamber of commerce will have future population estimates.

Real estate brokers will have land cost estimates, for the past, present and future. If you tell one or two local brokers that you are studying park needs, you should have no trouble getting help.

The park district should have its own plan with estimated needs and estimated costs. Certainly the park district secretary will have records of past land costs and acquisitions. If the park district does not have a plan or estimate of needs up to ten years from now, it would be a good idea to start forming one.

As you chart the future, plan beyond the obvious. Plan not only for organized team needs, but also for the unorganized boys who want to have a pick-up game.

When searching for land, ask yourself, where can children climb trees or run up and down hills? Where can anyone ride a bicycle safely? Where are the green spaces needed to relieve the crowded city appearance?

Some people at present feel that cities are outmoded. Certain cities seem to be fighting for their lives. Their survival will depend in a large part on how far the park board of each city looks ahead.

3

Recreation and
the challenge of leisure

DID YOU KNOW THAT HALF the deaths in this country are caused by heart and circulatory diseases which can be forestalled by active recreation involving healthful exercise?

Every city needs a strong and independent recreation board before it can begin to enjoy healthful benefits. There are examples of recreation programs run by a board with other responsibilities as well, but the price is high. The board members too often have no time for their own recreation.

Plan to initiate a recreation board or its equivalent in your city if you don't have one now. Villa Park, Illinois, showed how persistence pays. After several unsuccessful attempts to form a park district, with each referendum losing, the village officials set up a temporary playground and recreation board.

Fig. 6

10 LEADING CAUSES OF DEATH IN U.S. — 1966

Rates per 100,000 estimated midyear population.

Diseases of heart*	371.2
Malignant neo-plasms	155.1
Vascular lesions affecting central nervous system	104.6
Accidents	58.0
Influenza and pneumonia	32.5
Certain diseases of early infancy	26.4
General arteriosclerosis*	19.9
Diabetes mellitus	17.7
Other diseases of circulatory system*	14.6
Other bronchopulmonic diseases	14.5

*Could be helped by exercise.

Source: U.S. Department of Health, Education and Welfare.

During the trial period, a full-time recreation director named Don Henkle started everything his budget could afford, from baseball to croquet.

By the end of a two-year trial, the voters could see enough to want more. A referendum for a permanent recreation board and a special tax passed. The demand was there — even in a town that had repeatedly turned down earlier elections for a park district.

Ideally, the recreation director should be a qualified, full-time person. If the budget is limited, an effective program can be built by an exceptional part-time man. (A gym teacher will be on vacation when the needs are the greatest.)

The recreation board must be skilled in public relations. Any program will be more useful if many people hear about it. A referendum will pass more easily if enough voters have been reading and hearing about the board's accomplishments. All the news media should be notified about programs: radio, television, and the newspapers. Pictures in the local news-papers help make people aware of the programs and remember them, especially if their own children or neighbors are shown.

It is the recreation board, not the recreation director, that sets the policy about what programs will be offered. The recreation director will have plenty of suggestions, but the board members should also be encouraged to develop their own ideas.

How can you expand the recreation program without adding more land? Chapter 2 explained how to get more land, but there are ways of growing no matter how much or how little land you control.

Secret is in programming

The secret is to program activities that don't use the playground and park land. The possibilities are almost endless. White Plains, New York, sponsors flying lessons at the local airport. Lombard, Illinois, rents the high school auditorium for its theatrical group. That theatrical group includes amateurs and a few professionals looking for more experience. A bicycle trip uses residential streets and forest preserve paths. Start as early in the day as you can, to avoid traffic. You might be able to organize a hiking trip for people who want to escape the congested part of the city, if you get bus transportation to a likely spot. A bowling alley manager who desires to line up future customers might give reduced rates to a young people's class in the afternoon. One owner included free bus trans-portation from the park to the bowling alley.

The recreation board can help amateur musicians get together. Take applications from people who seek others of equal ability. Have each person rate his ability from "A" to "D" on the application. The typical musician will not overrate himself, because he does not wish to be in a group where he will be outclassed.

How about a program for people who aspire to be writers but

who need help and encouragement? The Night Writers of Tulsa have had requests to join from as far away as Tel Aviv. This group is not sponsored by a recreation board, but there is no reason why a recreation board somewhere else shouldn't try it. Some experienced, published writers will give the group a professional touch, if you can induce them to cooperate.

Recreation in hospitals

People in hospitals need recreation very much but they usually receive very little. Recreation can speed recovery by brightening the patient's outlook, make his life interesting instead of boring, take his mind off his troubles, bring him together with other people and keep him from brooding himself into a chronic illness. It can even help a patient who needs to stay a while, by encouraging him to finish his treatment instead of going home too early.

The hospital administration should be able to help work out a schedule that will fit the hospital routine. Local organizations, including churches and civic groups, can furnish volunteers to serve free. Work by the volunteers can include wheeling a patient into the lounge, playing cards or checkers, organizing group games or songfests, and arranging outings.

The patients who benefit the most from hospital recreation are the ones who are in for the longest stay — people whose recovery is delayed by complications, worry, etc. Children particularly need fun, encouragement and relief from boredom.

There is another kind of specialized need that is winning recognition. Ten years ago, if you told the staff of a mental hospital that you were ready to establish a recreation program for the inmates, it would have thought you were a likely candidate for their services. Now that is changed. Today, mental hospitals not only recognize that patients have a right to recreation, but also that there is a healing value. It might be difficult, but not impossible, to enlist volunteers. A few cities are trying a halfway house program to help people who are about to be released. New York has Fountain House, Chicago has The Thresholds, and Minneapolis has The Circle F Club.

We know that the number of old people is increasing. The University of New Mexico has a graduate program in recreation for the aged. White Plains has recreation for people in nursing homes. The activities include easy games, and travel for those who can get away for awhile.

By default, local governments can lose part of their authority over senior citizens' recreation. There is a pilot federal program for community centers for old people. Federal aid is channeled through state welfare departments and then to local governments.

If there is no local government to accept the aid, a local civic group can agree to establish a senior citizens' center and secure the federal aid.

Fig. 7

Del E. Webb Development Co.

The need for recreation has no age limit. Healthful but mild physical activity can be provided in many ways for the elderly. For example, Del Webb's Sun City in Arizona offers an attractive shuffleboard court.

This is the kind of a program that can expand rapidly when national defense costs eventually taper off.

Most of the published advice about recreation for teen-agers ignores a persistent problem — a problem that has bitterly disappointed some sponsors. An individual or a group will organize a teen-age club for dancing and soft drinks. Everything goes smoothly for the first few weeks. Then a few teens bring hard liquor to the parking lot, fights erupt, and the dream of a wholesome place for the teen-agers is shattered.

Teen recreation dilemma

I don't have the answer. Perhaps the idea of a kind of a nightclub for teen-agers is wrong. Certainly much greater success has been achieved by the coffeehouse idea. A coffeehouse is a place for young people to meet and talk. Chess or checkers can be furnished. Sometimes a short movie or a lecture is presented. The idea is to provide an atmosphere where teens can think and talk as well as have fun.

Let your imagination soar to cultivate recreation ideas. San Carlos, California, has 4-H farms in the city for city youngsters. This means active participation by boys and girls, not just a zoo-like exhibit of farm animals.

The recreation department must face the problem of vandalism sooner or later. Recreation equipment and buildings appear to attract trouble from time to time.

As a minimum, a building should never be open without a recreation employee to watch it. You might find you can rely on adult leaders or team coaches to watch the building when their teams are in it, but most communities report better results when having a recreation employee in the building at all hours. For outside areas, you need a workman or a policeman either all the time or at unscheduled intervals. To reduce rough horseplay on the ice-skating lagoon, a uniformed policeman on ice-skates does more good than a chairborne patrol in the warming house.

Fig. 8

Recreation facilities for senior citizens need not be expensive. Lawn bowling is a popular game at Sun City, Arizona. This community, too, provides an elegant swimming pool and a golf course.

Often the most serious damage is done at night when the park, field house or swimming pool is closed. Volunteer help can be effective. In one midwest town, employees of the recreation department took turns staying up all night to detect the small group that was breaking into swimming pool lockers. The watchers did not need to apprehend the vandals; a timely call to the police was enough.

Another way to fight vandalism is to expand the recreation program. The effect of a widened recreation program on juvenile delinquency is difficult to measure, but anything that keeps boys interested in wholesome activities prevents crime and saves money. Recreation does not cost as much as crime.

Johnstown, Pennsylvania, has active programs for youth through the schools and other agencies. Johnstown also has a low crime rate: 328 serious crimes a year per 100,000 population, about one-tenth as much as Los Angeles. The youth activities must be given part of the credit.

A mistake that is made in recreation programs all too often is forgetting that public recreation is for the entire public. If your band director cuts everyone but the best players from the band, and if he has no "B" band for average players, he is not running a true public recreation program. Why should the parents be taxed for a band that their children cannot join?

This mistake crops up in team sports, such as baseball. Little League managers should organize a farm or minor league for boys who don't make the first team, making it possible for everyone to play. Since enthusiasts for a sport sometimes do not see this, the recreation board must be ready to point out the need as tactfully as possible.

Organized and individual sports

There is still another problem created by the emphasis on team sports. In a midwestern city, two boys broke into a school gym after dark. Their motive? They wanted to throw the basketball around and shoot a few baskets without joining a team. If they had been part of an organized team they would have been admitted to the gym on practice nights. No one thought of the boys who want to play without joining an organization.

Unorganized recreation is the most neglected field of recreation today. Children need time to learn to be independent. Some are not team minded. Others are overweight or not very skillful. They need recreation.

The Chicago Park District has field houses where there is free time for the use of equipment. The boys are not turned loose in the building without a caretaker, but they can use the facilities without a coach. Include the unorganized time as a part of your program as it is important enough to have a place on the schedule.

Lombard, Illinois, successfully combines organized activities with free time on its ice-skating lagoon. Even when a skating tournament is going on, part of the ice is for free skating.

Your recreation board needs help to operate these ambitious programs. There are several ways to get cooperation.

Topeka, Kansas, has a summer internship program for serious students of park and recreation administration. This kind of program is worthwhile only if the interns are assigned challenging, not routine, work.

College students can increase the staff during the summer when recreation programs are the most active. Arrange to have experienced help to operate the power equipment. Inexperienced personnel is much more likely to suffer injuries.

Cooperation stretches dollars

Cooperation with other local governments will stretch the recreation dollar. At Awada, Colorado, four governments work together: the Metropolitan Recreation and Park Districts, the County School Board, the County Board and the City Council. The advantages of sharing employees, equipment and land are obvious. The exact division of labor is worked out by agreement between the governing bodies. This takes advance planning, because equipment and land are bought for many years' use. Don't get discouraged if it takes a while to get started. See Chapter 2 for ideas about sharing land and equipment.

Most states have a park and recreation association that sends out a newsletter or magazine and holds meetings. The National Recreation and Park Association, 1700 Pennsylvania Avenue N.W., Washington, D.C. 20006, publishes information, calls regional conferences and holds a national conference once a year. The President's Council on Physical Fitness, Washington, D.C. 20203, has pamphlets on the need for active recreation.

Montgomery Ward has a movie called "Community Action for Recreation." To borrow it, write Educational Services,

Public Relations Department, Montgomery Ward & Co., Chicago, Illinois 60607.

Chapter 13, "How to Pass a Referendum", tells how to mobilize public opinion to win an election to start a complete program.

Your city has the leadership and resources for a strong public recreation program — with your help.

Keep the recreation program up-to-date. If karate is popular in your city, find a qualified karate instructor. When something else wins favor, ride with the tide. Let people know that the recreation department is a vital force in your community.

4

Police can still

enforce the law

CRIME RATES ARE CLIMBING fast. Certain Supreme Court decisions sharply limit police methods which deny counsel for the accused. The increase of violence, civil rights protests, student unrest, and resistance to the draft are a worrysome problem. Officials responsible for law enforcement surely must be tempted to enter other occupations.

Still, a few cities are holding their own or, in some years, even reducing major crime rates.

The causes and prevention of crime are complex. No one knows for sure why one city has a higher crime rate than another. When a city manages to reverse the trend of rising crime, though, it must be on the right track. Local government can do, legally, many things that improve law enforcement.

The first and a fundamental step is to enlist the aid of the public. There is no such thing as law enforcement without public respect and cooperation. We can see this every week, everywhere from campuses to inner city areas.

In Chicago and Indianapolis, major crime rates have gone down during some recent years. Part of the reason is a vigorous program to enlist the public's help.

Signs and advertisements urge citizens to call the police whenever they see either a crime or a suspicious act. Sometimes a citizen will solve a case just by remembering a license number. Easy-to-read signs on motorcycles and squad cars show the police telephone number. Tucson, Arizona, and Kansas City, Missouri, also use this method. The battle is to overcome public apathy, and bring citizens to the side of law and order.

Public can help prevent crimes

Public information does more than help catch criminals. It can prevent crime. Recently six girls parked their car at a parking meter in the Old Town section of Chicago. They got out and locked their purses in the trunk. With a false sense of security, they went sightseeing. When they returned, the trunk was open and their purses missing. If they had listened to the police department's advice to never leave anything of value in a parked car, they would have prevented a crime.

City officials warn people to keep their cars locked and to remove the keys. This will not discourage the habitual car thief but it usually stops the joyrider. Many auto thefts are committed by a casual thief who can't, or won't, break into a locked car and start it without the key.

While people will call the police more often if they are urged, they won't engage in a fight to stop a criminal. A few years ago in New York, robbers and muggers declared open season on late night subway riders. Finally, New York assigned one policeman to each subway train between 8 P.M. and 4 A.M.

Fig. 9

FELONY CALLS BY TIME OF DAY, TYPICAL CITY

Shift	Sun.	Mon.	Tue.	Wed.	Thurs.	Fri.	Sat.
12 a.m.- 8 a.m.	12	9	9	9	9	10	17
8 a.m.- 4 p.m.	14	14	14	14	14	15	21
4 p.m.-12 a.m.	20	20	20	20	20	41	41

Source: Compiled by author from various cities' police reports, showing crime increases during evenings and weekends.

Felonies on subways did not cease but they did slow down, from 579 to 216 in one year.

Adding more policemen wouldn't have been enough; the city picked the most effective time and place for its additional men.

Atlanta, Georgia, had success with reassigning its men. Police were shifted from quieter times to the hours when most of the disturbances occur: Friday nights and weekends. Indianapolis holds a mobile unit in reserve to send into a trouble zone. Tucson has an electronic board that helps keep track of every police car, so that the nearest can be sent, regardless on whose beat the call is in.

Make a chart to show how you can check the hours when you need more policemen, and when a reduced force may be safe. You will probably find that you need more men on weekends, and fewer on weekday mornings, as was the case in Atlanta.

Modern conditions demand better-trained police. Police must know not only how to avoid violating the complex rights of the defendants under present Supreme Court rulings, but also how to collect effective evidence despite those rulings. A better-trained police force should also help, no doubt slowly, to improve the public image of lawmen.

Unfortunately, police training varies widely among cities. In some cities a policeman can be hired and assigned to the streets with no previous instruction. If the city isn't big enough to have its own police training school, it can work jointly with others, or arrange a tuition system with a nearby larger city. Some towns have frequent classes and invite other departments to enroll their new men.

Extra training is helpful to experienced law officers, too. Many police departments, colleges and law schools offer courses in police science and evidence. One of the cities that has reduced major crime in recent years, Indianapolis, gives courses to policemen both in police science and in public relations.

Certainly, it is difficult to attract well-qualified men to the police department at present, but any training that improves our law enforcement agencies will eventually raise the prestige of policemen.

The nation's colleges and universities can help the beseiged police departments. A few college men and law school graduates are now entering large city police departments. Some police departments are encouraging promising officers to study law while on the police force.

States are beginning to move to meet the need for police schooling. Missouri has a police school at Rolla. Illinois legislators passed a measure in 1965 to set up police schools throughout the state. The Federal Safe Streets Law provides aid for police training. It is not likely that changes of administration will affect the trend for federal help to strengthen local police departments.

Securing usable evidence

The confession rules established by the Supreme Court create a new training need. Even experienced policemen need a class or lecture to help them secure useable evidence.

As a minimum, a policeman must know that he cannot hear even a voluntary confession without first telling the suspect that he has a right to talk to a lawyer before he tells anything. The defendant must be booked, and bond set, as quickly as possible.

In spite of recent Supreme Court decisions, there are still ways to get a confession that will be right legally and morally. An effective policeman can obtain a confession without brute force. Detroit and Los Angeles report that they are getting as many indictments as they were before — but they're working harder at it.

Investigators — sympathetic or tough?

A good investigator can secure a confession by being sympathetic rather than threatening. Professor Fred Inbau of Northwestern University, author, lecturer and adviser to police, proved this when he was questioning a suspected wife murderer. Inbau encouraged the husband to talk about how difficult it is to get along with women. Finally he asked, "Where did you hide the gun?" This gave the husband an indirect way to get the whole thing off his chest: he described the spot in a vacant lot where he had thrown the weapon.

With an experienced criminal, sympathy may not work. Cold logic is more effective. I advise that police point out the flaws in his story, and do some leg work to check out his alibi. If you can show him that his story has little chance of convincing anyone, he may cooperate.

Be careful how you promise to work for a light sentence in return for cooperation. You may be promising something you can't deliver: check with your local prosecutor for his ruling.

It has always been true that a confession must be voluntary. Police cannot use force, the threat of force, or prolonged questioning to get a confession.

The new rules now require four essential warnings to be given to each suspect before questioning: (1) he has the right to consult a lawyer before he talks; (2) if he cannot afford a lawyer, the court will provide one at the expense of the state (or at the expense of the county); (3) he does not have to say anything and he can stop talking any time; (4) anything he says may be used against him.

Even though a defendant confesses voluntarily after being fully advised of his four rights, he might later change his mind. He may lie about the way the confession was obtained, to try to discredit it. Police can take legitimate steps to protect themselves from this kind of a lie.

One way is to invite a neighborhood businessman to hear the confession with the police. Some people are still willing to become involved. Of course, you won't be able to secure a businessman for every little case. If the accused later changes his story and claims that the confession was beaten out of him, the police will have a disinterested witness to back them up. This idea can be quite useful these days, when it is fashionable to believe even the most serious accusations against policemen.

The second way to protect the confession is to be ready to prove that the accused read it carefully before he signed, and that no pages were switched.

You do this by making sure there is at least one glaring mistake on each typed page of the confession. When the accused reads it, ask him to watch for typographical errors. Suggest that if he sees his name misspelled, a wrong address or an incorrect detail, he is to cross out the mistake, write in the correction in ink in his own writing, and initial the correction. There is no illegal coercion in this: it will keep the accused from trying to prove that he didn't read the confession before signing or that pages were switched.

Too many gambling cases are lost because city police sometimes do not get usable evidence.

1966 Tulsa case

Late in 1966, a policeman in Tulsa climbed a tree to peer into a house window. Seeing a dice game going on, he dived into the room through the window. At the trial, the judge pointed out that, while the officer meant well, he had no business doing a Batman act. The case was dismissed.

Police must get a warrant before forcing their way into a

gambling place for a search or an arrest. Usually there's plenty of time: the game will not break up early.

In a few cities, police make headlines by making spectacular raids, without a warrant. When the case comes up for trial, it is quietly dismissed.

Citizens' right to know

As a citizen or as a city official, you have a right to demand to know why the police failed to secure a search warrant. Failure to do the job of enforcing the law reflects on the entire city administration, not only on the police. Spectacular raids without warrants can be a subterfuge for illegal gambling while pretending to stop it.

An easy way to find out if there is undercover gambling going on in your town is to ask a cab driver to take you where the action is. He will readily comply. Organized crime cannot keep gambling hidden. Its profitability depends entirely on the public's ability to find gaming houses. Organized criminals are not too clever to get caught, even though they bribe susceptible public officials and police officers with money and favors.

In most communities, policemen cannot be fired without a civil service hearing. A great deal of misunderstanding surrounds these hearings.

First of all, when does a department call a policeman in for a civil service trial? Most departments will schedule a trial whenever a man is accused of anything that could result in firing him: neglect of duty, taking bribes, or beating up a person who was arrested. Ordinarily, the policeman's private life off duty is his own affair. For example, going bankrupt because of too many personal debts is not grounds for removal.

Second, the city officials need to remember that a policeman is entitled to a fair trial when he is charged with wrongdoing. He has a right to advance notice of what the hearing is all about. He can have his own lawyer. The lawyer for the civil service board cannot be prosecutor and judge at the same time;

there must be one lawyer to prosecute and another to advise the board of procedure.

Third, despite the practice in some circles, it is not wise to believe without question an accusation of police brutality. Cynical criminals have discovered that they can divert attention from their crimes by accusing the police of "brutality." A young police officer in New York has had to face such charges repeatedly, even though he always clears himself. Petty criminals remember his name, and when they are arrested, charge that he slugged them.

Many cities have a civil rights group of some kind. The way the city handles civil rights demonstrations can make or tarnish its reputation. Legally, the police do not take sides in a dispute. They merely make sure that there is no breach of the peace. This means that the rights of groups to parade, with a parade permit, are protected. It also means that the civil rights of a property owner or organization to keep unwanted demonstrators off their property must also be protected. Demonstrators who invade private property over the objection of the owner, and opponents who interfere with peaceful parading, are both impartially subject to arrest, as nonviolently as possible.

Riots vs. civil rights

A riot is not the same thing as a peaceful civil rights demonstration — it is the direct opposite. The rioters may ignore the civil rights of everyone in their path.

A riot is an irrational and violent situation, which can be brought under control only by fast, decisive, massive action. In most cases where police action was delayed, the result was a more severe riot, requiring eventually more massive police action to stop it. In the Watts incident in 1964, and others in 1967 and 1968, officials waited hours before calling the national guard. The rioters were not calmed by the lack of police. These became the worst riots of recent history. The situations went out of control during the hours that passed before the national guard was called.

To be ready for fast and decisive riot control action, the city officials must start planning their moves far in advance. Two of these plans include: (1) steps to reduce the conditions that lead to riots, and (2) steps to act quickly with manpower if a riot threatens. The first plan is the only real solution.

Fig. 10

Los Angeles Police Dept.

Police helicopters are used not only for traffic control, but also to keep dissident group activity in the streets under surveillance, and to track down criminals in open country.

Racial tensions are hardly likely to cease until black Americans have equal opportunities for jobs, wages, housing and education. We have also seen demands for local control in politics, schools, community affairs, and even in the matter of job selection and pay. These demands are understandable and justifiable.

College students request a voice in the selection of courses, professors, and in administration.

Young people want to control their destinies. They oppose the draft because their parents and others of the last generation started the wars. In fact, they appear to be against the whole Establishment — business men, clergy, teachers and so on; as well as against social customs, politics, welfare practices and the like.

Even comparatively wealthy suburban America is unhappy, demanding change in government policies, both domestic and foreign. They want an end to lawlessness and inflation.

All of these problems must be solved. Only then will we have true law and order.

When dissident groups gather to protest, they are confronted by the police. The police, to them, represent what they are against. Hence, they vent their anger and fury against lawmen.

Obviously, the ideal policeman would have to be a welfare worker, a psychologist and a clergyman to discharge his duties capably. Instead, he may have anything from a rather limited education to a college degree or two. Even his police training may require only a few weeks. It's no wonder that the police have a difficult time maintaining law and order. Perhaps it is unrealistic, too, to ask a police officer to remain cool and poised when he is cursed, spat upon, and attacked with clubs, bricks and garbage by a furious, unreasoning mob. Still, police must have a short term plan.

Over-reacting

Today the danger is that officials will over-react to rioting. The duty of officials is to stop rioting, and to use no more force than necessary. Also it is the duty of officials to work for equality of opportunity for everyone, regardless of color or political belief.

Continue to build constructive programs for minority and dissident youth groups, without placing the city in the position of seeming to reward rioters. Remember, the rioters and the inciters weren't elected to represent the people and they don't represent most of them unofficially either. The elected representatives, men who are sworn to uphold the Constitution and the law, are the real spokesmen for all Americans.

Some effective plans can be made ahead of time for riot

control. Know whom to call, and the telephone number of the national guard if it's needed. Know how long it will take for the guard to assemble and reach the troubled spot. On a peaceful day, meet the men who command the troops.

In the summer of 1967, Tampa, Florida, enlisted the aid of Negro youths to help control riots. If young men in potentially explosive neighborhoods could be recruited ahead of time for riot duty, there would be at least two advantages: First, an effective force would be ready to meet the emergency. Second, and perhaps more important, a part of the same neighborhood would be prepared to discourage rioting.

New York uses busses to move policemen around quickly in a rioting neighborhood. When the mob turns down a street, the police enter the bus and speed to a corner to cut it off. This system turns the mob back again and again. Each time the crowd is turned, a few people become tired or discouraged, and its size dwindles.

Local civic leaders can help by going into the disturbed area. If trouble has been stirred up by racists, use discretion and induce black civic leaders to help quell the rioters.

Your city can't use past history to predict if there will be a riot now or later. Plan now and be ready.

Crime-fighting technology

All phases of police work, from traffic control to crime detection, are changing because of the technological revolution that we're having. However, this will not end the shortage of policemen. Under our present conditions of disrespect for the law, we need an increasing number of men. A generation ago one policemen per one thousand population seemed adequate; now it's two policemen per one thousand. Although good equipment can never replace good policemen, it can help them cover more ground.

A man on foot can't cover as much territory as a man in a car, but a man in a car can't see what's going on as well as a man on foot. Especially from the driver's seat, a policeman doesn't know what's going on in the second story and in back yards. On a motor scooter or a miniature motorcycle he could see as well as a man on foot, and travel about as fast as a man patrolling residential neighborhoods in a car. If necessary, he could rush down a driveway or even a walkway quickly.

New York assigns motor scooters to patrol public parks. I'd like to see an enterprising suburb somewhere in the United States try motor scooters for patrolling residential areas. For traffic control at night, the motor scooters wouldn't be as safe, but for most routine patrol purposes they would be more effective. The man on the scooter could see things that the man in the car would overlook. One squad car could be kept on duty and the remaining policemen could be on scooters. Small radios are available with enough range to cover the entire city.

Long Beach, California, uses a plainclothes bicycle patrol. This novel idea has proved to be a strong deterrent to serious crime in areas where it has been tried. Any man on a bike could be a policeman, so a criminal can never feel secure. Serious crimes in the area patrolled have gone down five per cent.

Radar and electric timers

Wary drivers have learned that radar and electric speed timers are widespread. Radar usually requires two policemen. One measurers a car's speed, then radios ahead for the second man to stop the speeder. Some judges have ruled that both policemen must come to court if the speeding charge is contested. Your city attorney can tell you whether you need two witnesses or one.

Electric timers are not the same as radar. A policeman who uses electric timers puts two tapes across the road, thirty-three feet apart. A car crossing the tapes starts and stops a stopwatch. The stopwatch is set in a dial that shows the speed directly: the longer the watch runs, the slower the speed indicated. This is usually used by an officer by the side of the road, during daylight hours, who can chase and wave down any speeder caught by the tapes.

For obvious reasons, the tapes are usually placed where they can't be seen from a distance, such as beyond the crest of a hill or where trees cast shadows on the pavement.

Larger communities can utilize other electronic aids effectively. Chicago has maps of the city on a series of consoles to help dispatchers send the nearest squad car to answer any call. This not only provides faster service to the public, but also makes existing men and cars go farther.

A department that has the electronic equipment to keep track of each car can use the fluid patrol system. This means squad cars don't have to stay in a specific beat or zone. Cars can be shifted from one part of the city to another whenever needed. For a medium to large city, this can be as good as having more cars and more men.

Chicago Police Dept. Fig. 11

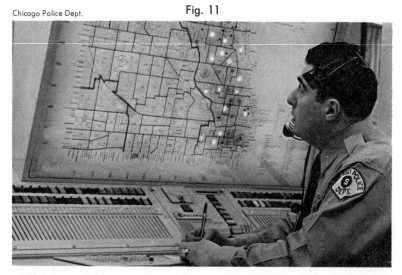

Electronic monitoring helps a police dispatcher direct assistance quickly where it's needed. The location of every patrol car is known at any given moment; hence, fewer cars can cover a greater area.

Electronic eavesdropping is a modern invention that is poorly understood. Many elected officials don't realize the dangers such equipment can create, because they don't know how these devices are used.

For example, investigators will break into a house when the owner is away and hide a small tape recorder in the bedroom. A week or two later, they return when the owner is away, break in again and take out the tape, which recorded everything their suspect said. They hope to pick up some leads that will help them in their investigation.

There is no way to limit the use of this kind of investigation to criminals. Any citizen who displeases any investigator can be the target. To the best of my knowledge, most of the charges of this type of invasion of privacy have been directed against federal rather than local officials. Local elected officials must stay alert to make sure that similar devices are not operated locally.

Checking up on organized crime

The usual justification for electronic eavesdropping is that organized crime is so strong that law enforcing officials need an extra advantage. The best answer to this is in your own back yard. List the locations where illegal gambling and vice are promoted by organized crime. If the criminal syndicate was unbeatable except by a huge, well-equipped law enforcement staff, there would be more organized crime in smaller towns than in big cities. Your list of locations of gambling spots probably will show, on the contrary, that a small town with a ten-man police force has no illegal gambling, while a big city with the latest equipment has all kinds of organized crime. Experience in this end of the law enforcement convinces us that local government's integrity, not its equipment keeps out organized crime.

Telephone tapping often is done and usually is denied. Certain ingenious telephone listening devices don't need a direct connection to the wires to be tapped. A pick-up is placed over the telephone wire to register electromagnetic impulses. This device is hard to detect. Usually, if your telephone is being tapped, you'll hear unusual noises, clicks and buzzes. Often there will be a reduced volume of sound. The local telephone company will send a repairman to check a complaint that a telephone is being tapped.

Police can't use as evidence in court anything they acquire by listening in on a private telephone conversation. Unfortunately, there is a way to get around this limitation: the information collected illegally can be used as leads to stronger evidence. This doesn't make the illegal act legal, but it does make it harder to stop.

Private conversations without a telephone can be overheard. There is a sound-focusing mirror that can be hidden in a truck. It can pick up a conversation in a house across the street. Another listening device works like a doctor's stethoscope: the end is held against the wall to detect sounds in the next apartment. This might evade the legal prohibitions against electronic eavesdropping, because the stethoscope is not electronic. The serious dangers that snooping equipment creates are not avoided, however.

Privacy, individual freedom, and the privilege to speak freely are a part of our way of life. No responsible law enforcement program can justify destroying these values just to bring in a crook or two.

Scientific aids to investigation have proved their value when used legally.

The so-called lie detector, or polygraph, is a time-saver that is often misunderstood. No light goes on and no bell rings when it catches someone in a lie. It merely shows symptoms which must be interpreted by an expert in this field. The polygraph measurers blood pressure, breathing, heartbeat and discloses whether a man's palms are sweating.

The first step in the use of the polygraph is to secure the

consent of the suspect. Reassure him that if he is innocent, he can use the machine's findings to clear himself, and that the man operating it is experienced and has a good record of accuracy. (If the operator is not expert, the test shouldn't be given at all.) The operator will make up a list of ten questions for the suspect. Some will be routine questions which the man will answer truthfully. One may be a control question that he will be likely to lie about, perhaps based on something in his past. This provides the operator with a pattern for judging the remaining answers. Usually, if the polygraph indicates the suspect is guilty, the operator can induce him to admit it after the test. Countless hours of checking false alibies or searching for evidence against the wrong man can be saved.

The drunkometer

A drunkometer is an aid to proving intoxication. The police officer needs the consent of the arrested man before he can give a drunkometer test. In fact, such a test would be impractical without cooperation, unless you could somehow persuade the man to blow up a balloon. A skillful approach to a belligerent drunk is to say, "If you're sober enough to drive, you can easily prove it," then hand him the balloon to blow up. More than one driver has regretted accepting this challenge.

The drunkometer measures the amount of alcohol in the suspect's breath, and from that a table indicates the presumed amount of alcohol in the blood. Many statutes state that a certain amount of alcohol in the blood raises a presumption of intoxication. This is never enough proof by itself. The arresting officer and the man who conducts the test must also testify about the condition that the suspect was in. They can refer to their notes to refresh their memories before trial, but they should be able to testify without reading directly from the notes. If necessary, the prosecutor can have them look at their notes while they're on the stand, then put them away and testify. Some departments have printed cards with a check list of what to look for as signs of intoxication, such as odor of alcohol, staggering, condition of eyes, incoherent talking, inability to tell what time it is and lack of orientation as to where he is or what's happening. Schools for police training and colleges occasionally have training courses for policemen on the use of the drunkometer.

Neighboring police departments can multiply their effectiveness by working together. Barrington Hills, Illinois, paid nearby Barrington to send a squad car to investigate serious crimes, and used its own cars for routine patrols. Chicago furnished training and a dog when nearby Hanover Park wanted to try out a K-9 corps. St. Louis County contracts with city police departments in the county.

Cooperation between police departments provides good service without a large consolidated force. A smaller police department has the advantage of being closer to the people. Preventing dishonesty in the smaller department is usually easier. In former President Johnson's 1967 State of the Union message, he mentioned our tradition of keeping police under local control.

Federal aid to local police

Federal aid to local police is a reality. The Office of Law Enforcement Assistance has more requests for aid than it has money available to provide it. There will be pressure for additional federal grants for preparing local plans and training programs. The trend to more and more federal aid to local government will no doubt result in more aid to police departments in the future. The problem will be to keep the police departments local. Federal aid must not create federally-controlled police. The best way to have honest, reliable police who respect citizens' rights is to have police managed by honest, reliable local officials.

What are some of the new ideas that will be used in future police work? Closed-circuit television is used right now in banks and shops to detect robberies or shoplifting. The same idea would work in parks, train stations and troublesome street intersections.

Today homeowners and businessmen can buy a sophisticated electronic system that will detect an intruder and notify the police through a taped message.

Claremont, California, uses a computer to store information from each beat. Computers could be programmed to help predict where and when certain kinds of crimes are most likely to happen. Incidently, Claremont keeps down costs by sharing computer time with the local school board.

Wichita Falls, Texas, reports that air conditioned cars and power steering help keep the men refreshed and alert.

Mace, a disabling gas which is supposed to have no harmful after-effects, may prove a useful substitute for guns in some circumstances. A policeman could not use Mace safely against a gunman, because it requires about five seconds to take effect — enough time for the officer to get shot.

A fast data processing system could compare the license number, physical description, and method of operating, with its memory bank, and identify a thief before he had time to hide the loot. Now, by the time the necessary files are checked, the guilty party has had hours or days to conceal himself or hide evidence.

More publicity for heroic police would help improve the policeman's image. This would have two benefits: it would inspire the public to be more cooperative when the police need information, and it would help in recruiting qualified men.

No device or system will replace the most effective police weapon of all: a career man in uniform, backed both by elected officials and the public.

5

Local streets and traffic

Salt lake city, utah, planned for the automobile fifty years before it was invented. In 1848 the pioneers laid out the city, boldly creating main and side streets that were six lanes wide. Since that time Salt Lake City, like other cities, has accepted much narrower streets, with results that might be expected.

In Los Angeles, about one-third of the real estate is taken by streets. In all cities, wider streets and new expressways are displacing homes and businesses. The population is increasing and so is the number of cars per family. Chapter 6 shows how some of the strain can be eased by mass transportation, but the number of cars will continue to increase. Figure 12 shows the fast rate of increase in publicly and privately owned cars and trucks, except military vehicles. The trend is clear. This is why you can usually spot the street commissioner in a group of city officials: he's the one who looks like he's on the verge of hysterical laughter.

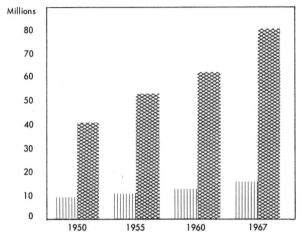

Fig. 12
INCREASE IN NUMBER OF VEHICLES
1950-1967

The column on the left is for trucks and buses, the higher column on the right for each year is for private cars.

Source: Transportation Association of America.

Actually, streets can be handled without confusion, but this requires a reexamination of the fundamentals.

By fundamentals I mean not only laying out a wide enough right-of-way in the first place, but also providing the kind of pavement that will last, buying pavement at the best possible price with honest bids and reliable workmanship, and planning new streets with vision, so they won't be overloaded from their first day of service.

Fundamentals also include providing sufficient off-street parking, not token off-street parking, and having places for pedestrians to walk safely without interfering with the travel flow. Street planning means coordinating large metropolitan centers with mass transportation facilities. Attempts should be made to pass zoning regulations which discourage concentration of business and industry locations in a crowded downtown area.

Public support for the street program is a basic necessity.

Begin by planning for a wide enough right-of-way. The street right-of-way is wider than the street pavement. It includes all the land that the city owns at the side of the pavement: the sidewalk, any parkway between the sidewalk and the street, and usually one foot of ground on the side of the sidewalk away from the street. It can also be used for sewer mains, water mains, and storm water drainage. When the street is first laid out, enough right-of-way must be planned for any future expansion that might be needed. The cost of land on which buildings are erected can be prohibitive for street use.

The way to decide how wide a right-of-way is needed for a proposed street is to study the overall plan for the development of the neighborhood and the city. Will the area have single family homes, apartments, offices, stores, schools or factories? Will the street be used immediately or in the foreseeable future for through traffic? Until you decide these questions, the width of the right-of-way can't be figured.

Chicago has a typical, growing American city's traffic conditions. Figures 13 through 16 are patterned after Chicago's streets but simplified to show the principle involved. The actual streets always must be altered a bit to meet local conditions. Figure 13 shows how cars and trucks can move from expressways to United States and state highways and to arterial streets. Figure 13 also shows the individual residential streets that have access to the arterial streets.

As few residential streets as possible join arterial streets in sound street planning. This minimizes slowing down of traffic and dangers of accidents. The location and size of the arterial

Fig. 13

EXPRESSWAY AND ARTERIAL STREET ACCESS THROUGH A CITY

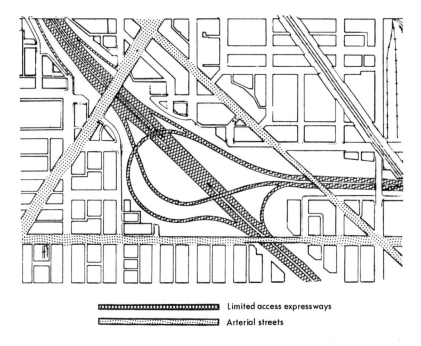

▓▓▓▓▓▓▓▓▓▓▓▓▓▓▓▓▓▓▓▓▓ Limited access expressways

▒▒▒▒▒▒▒▒▒▒▒▒▒▒▒▒▒▒▒▒▒ Arterial streets

streets depend on the amount of population and business to be served.

When planning arterial streets, remember that populations are increasing, the number of cars owned per family is growing, and what looks ample today may be too narrow in a few years.

Two contrasting ways to lay out residential streets are the gridiron pattern and the curvilinear pattern. In the gridiron pattern, straight streets are laid at right angles to each other. Figure 14 shows how this pattern fits into the arterial streets in one part of the area shown on Figure 13. This pattern uses less land for streets than any other, and it is easier for a stranger to find an address. One disadvantage of the gridiron pattern is that too many residential streets extend into arterial streets,

Fig. 14
GRIDIRON PATTERN

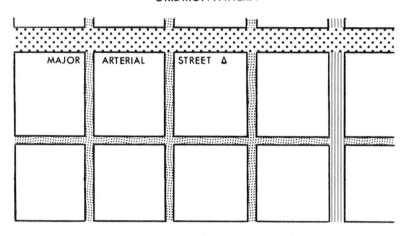

Fig. 15
GRIDIRON PATTERN WITH LIMITED ACCESS

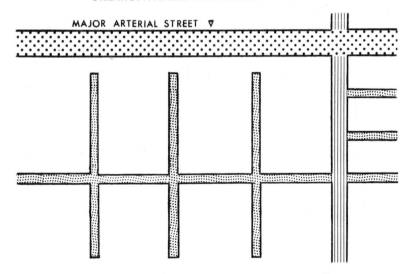

This pattern frees the major arterial street from cross traffic except at its intersection with the minor arterial street.

but this can be prevented by the modification shown in Figure 15.

The system that contrasts with the gridiron is the curvilinear pattern. Figure 16 shows a curvilinear pattern, usually seen in city residential areas. The major advantage of the curvilinear pattern is a varied, pleasing appearance. Street layout can take advantage of any natural attractions, such as a river or a bluff. This adds to the land costs, but it seems to encourage more imagination in the design and placement of homes on the lots. In earlier times we felt that curvilinear streets tended to slow down traffic in residential areas. This is still true for most drivers, but some fail to notice that the street is winding.

Fig. 16
CURVILINEAR PATTERN

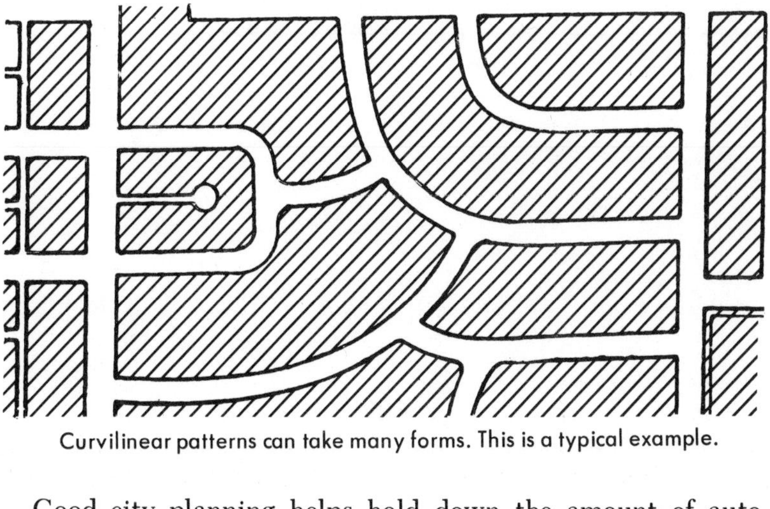

Curvilinear patterns can take many forms. This is a typical example.

Good city planning helps hold down the amount of auto traffic using the arterial streets. Figure 17 might look like a downtown business district, but it isn't. It's the pattern of an outlying shopping and commercial center such as might be part of an area shown in Figure 13. The center has shops, a bank, offices, large and small stores, restaurants, and a movie theater

Fig. 17
COMMERCIAL AREA

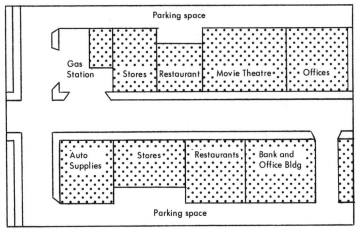

A shopping center with a wide variety of services does not have to be in the heart of the downtown area. This one is over five miles from the heart of Tulsa. Thousands of such centers are commonplace throughout the country today.

which serve the southeast part of the city. Residential areas surround it. Anyone can walk to work or drive a short distance. People will drive from many neighboring areas to work or shop at the center.

This is the type of city planning that does more for traffic relief than an expansion of the central business district. The latter only increases traffic and parking problems. Developing neighborhood business centers will not solve all problems, but it will help. Chapter 14, "Planning Is Dreaming," suggests how to create and use a city plan to coordinate traffic planning and to improve the use of land throughout the city.

With this in mind there are certain minimum right-of-way widths that city officials must require. For an arterial street, one hundred to one hundred twenty feet is the minimum. For a secondary street that will channel traffic into the arterial street, eighty feet may be enough. A residential street must have at least fifty or sixty feet.

Fig. 18

Public service facilities gobble up huge chunks of once-vacant land. Note how much of this St. Louis area is devoted to the Daniel Boone Expressway and interchange, public park with baseball diamonds, planetarium, lakes, and other facilities.

Freeways and expressways are in a class alone. Local officials don't ordinarily plan these directly, but they do work on them in two ways. First, the local officials work with the state and federal highway officials in the early planning and public hearing phases of the expressway in order to find the most effective location. Second, local access, secondary streets and arterial streets can be planned around the expressway interchanges.

Two ways to obtain a street right-of-way are: the land is dedicated without cost to the city; and, the city buys the land.

Most city streets are dedicated to the city without cost. The city can require, in its ordinances on new subdivisions, that the subdivider or land developer dedicate land for street purposes. In order to be sure of getting the minimum width that the city needs, the city officials must have an ordinance specifying the minimum widths for residential, secondary and arterial streets. The city attorney can advise whether the minimum width requirements are reasonable and valid for the state and the particular locality. If there is no ordinance on the subject, there is no way to make the subdividers grant the minimum width needed.

The other way of getting a street is by buying the land. If the property owner is willing to sell, and the parties can agree on the price, the land purchase is by contract like any land purchase. If the owner is unwilling to sell, or if the parties can't agree on the price, the city can still buy the land. This is done through a condemnation proceeding, also called an eminent domain proceeding. The city files a case in court to have a jury decide what the land is worth. The jury can't take into account the fact that the property owner doesn't want to sell. The only issue for the jury is the market value of the land.

Both the city and the property owner can call appraisers and real estate brokers to present their opinions on the land value. Then the jury decides.

After the land is purchased, the next step is to pave it.

The lowest initial cost is not the deciding factor. For example, a curb and gutter add little to the cost of the street, yet they can double the life of the pavement. They help protect the pavement from frost damage, which comes from water seeping under the street in the winter, and repeatedly freezing and thawing. Heavy traffic during a thaw will add to the damage. The street will cost less per year of its life if the pavement is made to last.

The kinds of pavements range from concrete pavements with a thick, strong base; blacktop or bituminous pavements also with a thick, strong base; to gravel pavements with little base. Some knowledge of the alternatives can save money at bid opening time.

For many situations, the city engineer will suggest that either a blacktop or a concrete pavement will serve equally well. He can prepare specifications covering all details such as the size of the crushed stone in the base course and the thickness of the pavement for blacktop; and another set of specifications for concrete pavement.

Calling for bids

When the city officials call for bids, they ask for bids in the alternative: contractors can bid on the concrete only, the blacktop only, or both. Local conditions or temporary problems of supply may make one or the other lower in cost. The city officials will be able to see, when they open the bids, which is the lower in cost.

After the bids are opened, the contract usually is placed with the lowest responsible bidder. Sometimes cities will use a subterfuge or technicality to take a bid away from the low bidder. The city officials might act in good faith, and think that they must reject a bid even for the most minor of flaws. An Illinois village found out too late that taking the second low bidder is not necessarily wise. The fact that the low bidder was much less experienced than the second low bidder caused the village to award the street contract to the latter. The officials feared that an inexperienced man might have trouble finishing a big project. After the second lowest bidder started the work, he began to argue with the village board about the manner of figuring the payment due. In the dispute, the workers were pulled off the job and the street was left unfinished.

Finally the village board was forced to hire another contractor to finish the project at a higher price.

Most experienced city fathers award the work to the low bidder regardless of any technical objections made. For example, if a bid is not signed, they allow the contractor to come to the front of the meeting room and sign when it is opened.

After the bid is let, the contractor starts work. From time to time, he sends a bill to the city and is paid for part of his work. Usually the contract provides for around ninety per cent of the value of the work done to date to be paid and for ten per cent to be held back until the entire street covered by the contract is finished.

Most street building contracts call for payment on a unit price basis. This means that, instead of a flat agreed price for the entire job, the contractor is paid so much a square foot for concrete pavement, installed; so much a lineal foot for storm sewer required by the blueprints; a stated price for each inlet and catch basin; and so on. The payments that are made while the work is going on are based on the unit price for the parts actually finished. For example, the city engineer will figure the amount of square feet of pavement finished, multiply by the unit price, and deduct the ten per cent reserve. The city council will approve payment of that figure.

The city engineer cannot certify to the amount of work done unless his inspector is at the site of the work at all times. Part of the price depends on things that are underground, such as fill for low places. He can't tell by looking at the surface of the ground whether there are storm sewers wherever they belong. Human nature being what it is, it's unsafe to rely on what the contractor's employees say.

Quality counts too

Not only is it a question of the amount of work done, but also a question of the quality of the work. The engineer has no way of knowing this unless he has had a reliable inspector present throughout the work. Is the pavement as thick as the plans require? Are the joints in the storm sewer carefully sealed? Was all loose material removed before the work started? The inspector must know.

In a midwestern city, some lightly-travelled residential streets began developing holes after they were only two years old. Investigation showed that the contractor had no solid base for the pavement. He had used old automobile parts to fill in some low spots. Either the city engineer's inspector wasn't there or he was given an inducement to overlook the violations.

By the time the defect was developed, it was too late to do anything practical. The city had approved the pavement two years earlier.

Whether the street pavement is installed on old streets by a contractor under contract with the city, or on new streets by a subdivider or land developer creating streets to be accepted by the city as city streets, the inspection problem is the same.

Checking up on the contractor

A city official doesn't need to be a technical expert to see if the inspector is permitting the contractor to use old auto parts for fill. One of the city officials ought to take the time to find out what's going on at the job site. An elected official, such as the commissioner or committee chairman in charge of streets, should do the checking.

If you are a city official, your presence can accomplish a lot at the job site. Tell the workmen who you are and ask for the engineer's inspector. If he is there, he probably will welcome your interest in the project. If he isn't available, ask where he is and make it a point to see him as soon as possible. Find out if he is on a coffee break and if he is often away. Come back a number of times. Make sure the inspector is usually there.

Look for glaring errors that you can correct while at the site. Measure the pavement for thickness. Does it comply with the specifications? Are the materials for city work finding their way onto private parking lots? If you spot no serious errors, if the city engineer's inspector is present, and if the inspector has a good reputation, your work is easy. Be genuinely interested and drop by unannounced from time to time to observe how the work is progressing.

City engineer's duties

This doesn't mean that the elected officials should take over the job of the city engineer or his inspectors. The city engineer, whether he's a full time employee or a consultant working for other clients beside your city, has the duty of making certain that the contractor fulfills the work contract. The elected city officials pay out the money, however, and they should make a definite effort to know what is going on.

Most elected officials have limited time. There's no need to be on the job constantly. Just call on irregular occasions, so that everyone knows you might show up at any time. Granted that you're not an expert on streets, you can be an expert on watching the experts.

For those streets that are not built by a subdivider or developer at his own expense, the city has two ways to pay the land and construction costs. Usually there isn't enough cash on hand to pay for the pavement. The cost must be financed.

If the street benefits the entire city, the city might issue general obligation bonds. These bonds are paid over a period of years, out of the road taxes, gasoline taxes, or any other tax levied over the entire city. The bond houses or investors who buy the bonds put up the entire cost, and in return get their money back with tax-free interest, over the life of the bonds. Ordinarily the city must hold a referendum before it can sell general obligation bonds.

If the pavement will benefit only one part of the city, special assessment bonds can be issued. These are paid out of charges, or assessments, against the property along the street to be paved. Sometimes land not adjoining the new pavement but within a block or so of it is charged a smaller amount, for indirect benefits. When a pavement is laid by special assessment, the city can pay part of the cost as a public benefit. Some people who handle special assessments believe that some public benefits should be charged to the city in every assessment. The cost of the intersections for instance, may be charged to the city. If the pavement is wider than the immediate neighborhood needs, the cost of the added width also may be charged as public benefits. No referendum is needed for special assessment bonds.

Planning the location and width of streets, taking the bids, and making sure the work is done satisfactorily and paid for, is part of the work of the street commissioner, or chairman of the street committee. The other part is using imagination to suggest improvements, other than streets, to help relieve traffic load.

Off-street parking

An obvious way to reduce the number of cars on the streets is to have more off-street parking. It might be free or for pay. It might be privately or publicly owned. Free parking has a strong effect in getting cars off the streets; parking for a fee has a slightly lesser effect. Drivers making deliveries may double-park or park in a pay lot without paying a fee.

Most cities have an ordinance that requires anyone building a new business, office or factory to provide off-street parking. The ordinance must have standards to provide one car space for so many square feet of store, office, factory, or warehouse space. Determining how many spaces will be necessary for restaurant parking is an approximation at best. It's difficult to predict exactly how many employees or tables the restaurant may have.

The best way to determine what is a reasonable amount of parking to require in the ordinance is to find out how much is provided, based on area, in the new shopping centers, offices, and factories in your city. Often the city building department or the county tax assessor will have this information. If not, building owners or managers may have blueprints or plats that reveal the facts you seek.

Have you noticed how many new doctors' buildings have a parking lot that makes the patients pay? If the object is to get as many cars parked off the street as possible, and to remove temptations to double-park and park in a no parking zone, a free parking lot would serve better. Ask the city attorney if he thinks you could require free off-street parking in your ordinance.

The off-street parking requirements of the ordinances cannot easily be applied to old stores, offices and factories that are already in existence. This is usually a problem in downtown areas, where privately owned parking garages or lots try to help.

Chicago's Loop

Chicago's downtown area, the Loop, exemplifies one of the problems of finding the right location for off-street parking. About six blocks square, the area is ideal for perimeter parking; that is, permitting parking around the edge of the Loop and having no parking within it. Unfortunately, the city wasn't planned that way. Parking lots are scattered throughout the Loop. Some are even owned by the city. Cars that could have been parked at the edge, letting their passengers walk to their destination, drive into the heart of the congestion. Try driving through the Loop during busy hours any weekday. Actually, the problem is typical of most cities.

An attractive solution to downtown traffic problems was planned about two thousand years ago. When England was part of the ancient Roman Empire, London city planners proposed separate levels for pedestrian and vehicular traffic.

Vehicles would move faster, without a mob of pedestrians at every corner. Pedestrians would walk in more safety and quickly without the vehicles. Turning vehicles would not delay traffic waiting for pedestrians to finish crossing with the right-of-way.

The basic idea was to have pedestrians on a different level from the vehicles. Pedestrians were to be on the surface, and the vehicles underground. The entire width of the street was to be used for walking and for an attractive planting strip. The vehicles also were to use the entire street width, including the part usually taken by sidewalks. Shops were to be located on the same level with the pedestrians. Deliveries were to be made on the lower levels. The project would pay for itself in increased business. London didn't try it, however. We're still waiting for some city to.

Public support is needed

Public support for such a program would be needed. People who must relocate to make way for a new street or expressway are unhappy about the street program. Whenever it's necessary to assess a special assessment for a street, even those who stand to benefit most are often the most discontented.

Successful public relations begins with efficient service and finishes with modest boasting.

If the city can prove that a project had been worthwhile and well executed, it should spend time and money to publicize the success.

City officials who keep holes in the streets repaired and remove the snow as quickly as possible have something to chortle about. In Berwyn, Illinois, a former public works commissioner, when there was much snow to remove from the streets, ran a tractor himself to ease the situation.

Keep street department in public eye

Keeping your municipal street department in the public eye is good public relations. Inform the newspaper, radio and television reporters when you start a new program. Tell them who will benefit and why it's needed. Whenever you're planning a street improvement anywhere (not only when required by law), hold public hearings. Write invitations to the people paying taxes on the property along the new pavement. Let everyone know what your plans will do for them.

A few years ago, traffic in Boston came to a virtual halt because too many people tried to use the same streets at the same time. Chicago and other cities have arrangements with radio stations to broadcast live traffic reports from a police officer patroling in a helicopter. Congestion is reduced by suggestions of alternate routes. Even without a trafficopter, cities can enlist the aid of the police and the local radio stations to warn drivers away from overloaded streets. This is one way to stretch the precious streets we have.

In Figure 12, the chart shows the increases in the number of cars and trucks on the road every year. Figure 19 shows a typical city. Make a similar chart for your city. Motor vehicle registration figures are available in your library. What will the figures be in five years? In ten? Consider what you'll need to do to be ready.

Fig. 19
REGISTERED VEHICLES IN HONOLULU, HAWAII

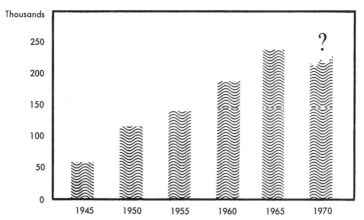

Source: City Clerk, Honolulu, Hawaii. These figures show taxable vehicles only. Many other American cities show a similar increase pattern.

If Salt Lake City planned one hundred years ahead for today's traffic, any other city can plan ten or twenty years ahead.

6

Mass transportation

by rail, water and air

Could your city use a means of transportation that would take up one-fifth as much space as an expressway while it carries three times as many people? Figure 20 compares expressways with a commuter railroad.

Metropolitan areas that have expressways have found that the expressway is not the whole answer to their problems. Statistics don't tell as much as a rush hour trip can reveal. Cars average about twenty miles per hour on some peak rush hours on expressways. Others, including occasional stops, average down to twelve miles per hour, the speed of a horse and buggy.

The problem is that the use of expressways reaches peaks twice a day, and there is no practical way in most urban

Fig. 20
COMPARISON OF COMMUTER TRANSPORTATION

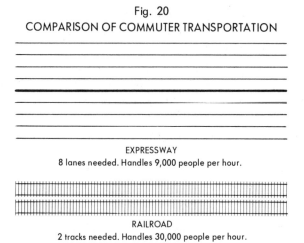

EXPRESSWAY
8 lanes needed. Handles 9,000 people per hour.

RAILROAD
2 tracks needed. Handles 30,000 people per hour.

Number of people per hour and amount of land required, expressways and commuter railways.

Source: Chicago Transit Authority.

centers to build enough roadways to carry all the traffic smoothly. No on wishes to pave the entire city, because then we'd have to erect buildings underground or on stilts.

The Eisenhower Expressway, serving the west side of Chicago and the western suburbs, has part of the solution. The expressway's eight lanes of auto and truck traffic have a capacity of 6,000 cars, or about 9,000 people per hour. In the median strip are two tracks of the Chicago Transit Authority's electric railroad. Its maximum rush hour traffic is 30,000 people, over three times as many as the expressway. Figure 20 compares the parts of the system.

The Chicago Transit Authority doesn't have planning jurisdiction over every type of transportation in the area. Still, an overall plan has developed, partly because of ideas independently worked out by private industry and the CTA. Several things happened, starting in the late 1940's and the early 1950's, to bring this about.

Primarily, the Chicago Transit Authority took over several existing independent transportation systems, combining all city bus lines, street car lines, elevated trains and subways into one ownership and management. Next, the number of stops on the elevated lines were reduced, on the theory that the shorter trips could be handled by busses and street cars. Later, street cars were eliminated and the entire city converted to bus and trolley-bus transportation coordinated with elevated and subway lines.

Meanwhile, the Chicago and North Western Railway, an independent business corporation, had been running three lines through the city, with a number of passenger stops, in some cases less than a mile apart. These railroad lines brought daily commuter traffic from as far away as Waukegan, thirty miles to the north, Crystal Lake, forty-two miles to the northwest and West Chicago, thirty-five miles to the west, to the central part of Chicago. Some of the trains made many stops within Chicago.

At the same time that the CTA was consolidating its lines, the Chicago and North Western Railway announced that it would eliminate many intermediate stops in the area amply served by the CTA. The railroad filed an application with the Illinois Commerce Commission and the Interstate Commerce Commission, seeking permission to close Chicago stations that had been open for generations.

Convinced by the railroad, the commerce commissions approved the proposal to close the stations. The railroad now had its downtown station, and intermediate stops reduced to a minimum.

In 1953 a competing electric railroad, the Chicago, Aurora and Elgin, lost part of its right-of-way and stopped giving direct service from the western suburbs to Chicago. This resulted in an increase in riders on the west line of the Chicago and North Western Railway, and suggested the unheard-of possibility of making money on commuter traffic. Since that time, the C&NW gradually converted its equipment to deisel engines, with double-decked air conditioned coaches specifically designed to handle commuter traffic.

Fig. 21

Chicago and North Western Railway

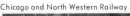

Private enterprise can solve part of the mass transportation problem. By converting to spacious, comfortable, air-conditioned trains, which move on time, the Chicago and North Western Railway serves commuters from Chicago suburbs without subsidy.

The C&NW is handling an impressive part of commuter traffic without government subsidies, yet earns a profit. This is evidence that a well-managed railway can cope with commuter transportation provided that coaches are modern, spacious and air-conditioned, and that trains run on time. Some lines are planning trains that travel more than double present speeds.

Many transportation authorities believe that all metropolitan transportation planning must be centralized in one agency. This includes not only roads and expressways for cars, commuter railroads and busses, but also airports, railroad, freight, truck routing, and the waterways. The Chicago situation shows that central control is not absolutely necessary; the various public entities and private businesses involved should each be able to handle their share of the planning.

Even without enabling legislation, overall planning for metropolitan transportation can be accomplished. Cooperation is the key word: Cooperation in pooling their existing plans, working jointly to state present needs and predict future ones, and joining with each other to perfect an overall workable plan. Cities and villages prove they can cooperate in other fields, such as police training programs and the sharing of police facilities or bringing water from a distant lake. See Chapters 4 and 7. A number of cities in a metropolitan area could appoint a joint study commission.

Some metropolitan areas now have transportation commissions provided for by enabling legislation with authority to plan for the future.

CTA and SEPTA

In Chicago, the Chicago Transit Authority is not an overall planning agency: primarily its agency operates bus, elevated and subway transportation.

On the other hand, in the Philadelphia area, the Southeastern Pennsylvania Transportation Authority has authority to plan the overall transportation for the four million people who live and work in this area.

The Southeastern Pennsylvania Transportation Authority, or SEPTA, has the job of coordinating the commuter transportation of railroads, subway and elevated lines, and bus lines. Its proposals include purchase of the existing Philadelphia Transportation Company, and efforts to make commuter railroads more effective.

To make existing commuter railroads more effective, fare schedules are revamped and city bus line fares are tied in with railroad fares. Subsidies will be sought for the commuter railroads. Commuter parking lots will be set up to make it easier to use the commuter railroads. The idea is working: commuter traffic on one segment jumped from 24,298 the first month to 33,910 the third month, on just one part of the system.

For every three new train riders, figure two cars will be off the road in peak hours.

Seeking to get the advantages of commuter railroads is San Francisco. That city is working to complete a new commuter railroad system.

About one-third of the real estate in Los Angeles is in highways, roads and expressways. Los Angeles has no commuter railroad transportation, and poor local service.

Without adequate mass transportation, a city cannot develop a clearly-defined downtown area. Without a clearly-defined downtown area, it is hard to start mass transportation. Los Angeles planners have recognized these interrelated problems. They will have to come up with a long-range solution.

Bus transportation by itself is only part of the answer. Buses

Fig. 22
HOW MUCH BULK CAN YOU SHIP FOR ONE DOLLAR?

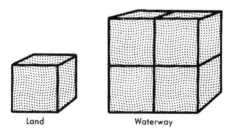

Land   Waterway

Bulk shipment means items such as grain or cotton. Actual costs vary, but the above comparison shows the great cost advantage of water transportation, using barges pushed by a tow boat, over rail or other overland transportation. Land shipment costs are roughly four times higher.

must use the expressways or other roads. Slow rush hour traffic slows down the buses. Scheduling stops is also a problem; the tendency is to have the bus stop so often that a trip of any distance takes much longer than an automobile trip over the same ground. Many commuters won't take the time to ride the slow, fitful bus. They drive if they can't take a train.

Most cities had a decrease in the number of bus passengers from 1966 to 1967. Dallas, Texas, had an increase, contrary to the trend. Dallas paid for the increase. The city subsidizes its bus line. Bus lines that operate without a subsidy are carrying fewer passengers. Dallas added more frequent service and managed to increase riders.

The question for local government is whether or not to pay the price of subsidizing transportation to increase the use of the bus line. If bus riders helped to remove congestion from the roads, there would be a strong case for the subsidy. It would be the same as increasing the street capacity by widening the streets. Obviously the answer will differ among localities. Study what's best for your city. Different problems of roads and expressways, and residential and commercial areas, require different solutions.

Look at other cities for comparative cost figures. Write cities near yours for the average cost per passenger, and the actual fare charged each adult.

A proposal that has been made from time to time, but never tested, is to have special expressways built for buses only. The idea would be to have an elevated right-of-way like the elevated tracks. So far no one has worked out a feasible, financially sound way of trying this.

General and commercial airports

Airports are an integral part of passenger traffic in all cities. The two distinct kinds of airport traffic, general and commercial, usually create congestion unless they are clearly separated.

General aviation includes privately owned planes and planes owned by corporations, but not scheduled airlines. While the greatest number of passengers ride scheduled airlines, many general aircraft use the busy airports.

If the busy airports with scheduled airlines, like O'Hare International in Chicago, the world's busiest, barred general aviation, there would be less congestion. The larger part of the traveling public would be served, and the danger of collision would be lessened.

General aviation is important to your city. To lure business you must attract general aviation, but offer an airport designed to be appealing, and limited to that use only.

One dramatic but effective proposal to cut air traffic congestion is to eliminate all general aviation at commercial airports. O'Hare discourages general aviation with a high landing charge. Changes in federal regulations will be needed to move general aviation away from the crowded airports. Although difficult to do, it can be done.

Fig. 23

Smaller cities interested in attracting business and industry should consider building a general aviation airport to serve private and company planes. New plants mean jobs, more money in the community, and a lucrative source of tax revenue.

Fig. 24
DISTRIBUTION OF TON-MILES
OF DOMESTIC INTERCITY FREIGHT TRAFFIC

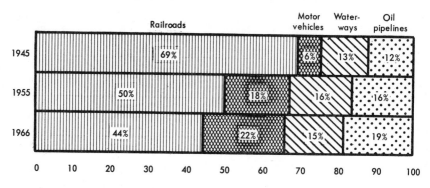

Source: Dept. of Commerce, Bureau of the Census. Data from Interstate Commerce Commission.

The main obstacle to removing general aviation from the crowded metropolitan airports will be the resistance of influential men who use it. The answer to this is to show these people how they will benefit from better air service if general aviation uses a safer field away from the main airport. Local governments can help by encouraging interest in an airport that serves general aviation only.

An airport for general aviation only can even help a city that doesn't have an airport for commercial airlines. When you weigh the value of a local airport, you understand that it will increase businesses other than the airport traffic.

It attracts the kind of businessmen who use planes for private purposes or to transport company people. New factories create jobs and generate a heavy flow of cash. If the local plant doesn't use the airport for air freight or regular business, the executives who fly will still justify its existence. It may be one of the factors that will determine if your community is chosen over other sites for new plants.

Many states have laws that allow a municipality to build its

Fig. 25
MASS TRANSPORTATION CHECK LIST

These are the author's opinion of the needs of Tulsa, Okla. Compare these with your city's requirements.

Kind of transportation	Available now?	Needed later?
Roads and highways	Adequate	More off-street parking
Expressways	Dangerous at peak hours	More required
Toll roads	None through the city	Could relieve expressways
Elevated or subway	None	Not required
Commuter railroads	None	These have been suggested for Tulsa and neighboring cities
Bus, local	Adequate since taken over by city transportation authority	Tax subsidies will probably be needed
Airports, air transportation	Adequate	Present airport can handle more traffic
Trucking lines	Adequate	Growth will require more trucks
Railroads, freight	Adequate	Railroads need to do more modernizing
Railroads, interstate passenger	Still used	Becoming obsolete
Bus, interstate	Adequate	Will be needed for foreseeable future
Water transportation (barges for freight)	Not available now	Needed for growth: scheduled to be completed in 1970

own airport. The municipality can issue bonds to pay the construction costs. Earnings of the airport, and possibly some tax money, can go toward paying for the airport construction. The problem, of course, is to see that the airport will pay for itself. Numerous states have provided for creating a local airport authority, a separate municipal corporation. The airport authority can sell bonds, buy land and build facilities, to be paid out of earnings.

Discovering whether or not an airport bond issue is feasible is like finding out whether any other kind of bond issue is feasible. Begin by estimating the taxes and earnings that the airport authority can expect during the life of the bonds. Then consult the experts: the city attorney, finance officer, and anyone who knows airport planning. Bond brokers and bankers may offer suggestions.

Water transportation attracts industry

For bulk shipping, the cost of waterway transportation can be one-fourth that of land transportation — quite a sharp difference. Some products can be shipped better by speedy air freight. Not all places are accessible to water transportation. Water transportation is ideal, though, for bulk shippers of coal, wheat, steel and the like. The city with good water transportation has a definite edge in attracting industrial growth.

The cities that can have waterway transportation may surprise you: if there is a river, shallow or deep, near the city, there may be hope.

The Arkansas River at Tulsa always was too shallow for boat or barge traffic. Still, there will be a Port of Tulsa by some time in 1970. The United States Army Corps of Engineers will dig out a channel and build dams to make an inland waterway along the Arkansas River. The first phases of the work improve the river through Arkansas to Fort Smith, near the Oklahoma border. Then the river will be widened and deepened up to where it meets the Verdigris River near Tulsa. The project continues along the Verdigris River to the Port of Tulsa, located a few miles east of the city.

Although this is a United States project, Tulsa officials helped make it possible. City planning provided for the necessary port facilities. The city worked on land acquisition. Some hard-fought condemnation cases ensued. The city put up two bond issues, one in 1966 for land costs and one in 1967 for building port facilities.

Another kind of waterway project helped Chicago a few years ago. The St. Lawrence Seaway Project deepened the channel of the 2,000-mile inland waterway through the St. Lawrence River and the Great Lakes to Chicago, enabling deeper draft ocean vessels to come all the way to that city. The metropolitan area of Chicago and the surrounding cities and villages continue to grow in population, in industry, and in land values.

Anticipating rapid growth from the benefits of its new waterway for tow boats and barges, Tulsa land developers are looking forward to increasing demands. See Figure 22.

If your city is near a river, start some long-range dreaming about the possibility of making it navigible. Write to your Senators and Congressmen in Washington. Find out if you have a chance for this kind of growth.

What are the mass transportation problems and opportunities in your community? What do you need for better freight transportation? Take stock. Use Figures 24 and 25 to compare what you have, what you will need, and what local, regional and federal agencies will be involved.

7

City services

increase property values

"OUR VILLAGE GOVERNMENT is so good you can afford to pay $3,000 more for a house."

A ridiculous claim? Let's look at what water service, fire protection, sewer service, garbage collection, cost control and cooperation with other communities can do.

For each $1,000 he owes on his mortgage, a home owner pays about $7.00 per month in mortgage payments. This means that if the village or city can reduce his cost of living by $7.00 a month, the municipality has given him a chance to pay off another $1,000 worth of home. Every $7.00 per month saved in water rates, taxes, insurance or commuting costs equals $1,000 worth of more home.

About a decade ago when Hanover Park, Illinois, was

organized as a new village, its officials insisted on a daring program of financing and building their own water plant. At approximately the same time a neighboring village let a commercial water company furnish water. The village's water rates in Hanover Park were set at $4.00 per month. In their neighboring village, the water bill was about $12.00 per month. The difference of $8.00 each month is more than enough to pay monthly payments on $1,000 worth of home.

Compare property taxes

Property taxes cost more than water. How much difference is there in real estate taxes on similar homes in different communities? The county treasurer's office has the total tax figures for the homes in the county. Pick out similar homes in a few different cities or villages and compare the taxes.

A difference of $168.00 per year is not unusual. Some similar homes have tax bills further apart than that. At $168.00 per year, this means that the home owner pays $14.00 per month. He could pay for $2,000 more worth of mortgage if he saved $168.00 a year in local property taxes. This is very practical, since the mortgage house ordinarily collects for the taxes, too. If the home owner's taxes were $168.00 lower he could get $2,000 more worth of house with identical monthly payments.

Although we've already saved the $3,000 we claimed by reducing water charges and local taxes, there are other ways to save. Better fire protection means lower insurance rates. If the sewers don't back up in the rain, hundreds of dollars worth of washing machines, furniture and hobby equipment in the basement won't be flooded and ruined. Home owners' insurance policies don't cover water damage caused by rain water. Doctor bills can be prevented with efficient garbage collection and disposal as well as with pollution regulations.

Obtaining a sound public works service and controlling the cost, then, has a very practical benefit.

Many municipalities near Chicago discovered that the best

way to get satisfactory water service is to buy water from that city. Figure 26 shows how water service to the suburbs, separate municipalities outside Chicago, increased for ten years while the total water used by the city and suburbs combined stayed about the same. The column, total pumpage, suburbs supplied, shows a steady growth in each year. The total number of suburbs served, and the population of suburbs served, also show a steady growth pattern.

Fig. 26
INCREASE IN COOPERATIVE WATER SERVICE,
CHICAGO TO SURROUNDING TOWNS.

Year	Total Pumpage Chicago and Suburbs Million Gallons	Total Population Served	Number of Suburbs Supplied	Total Pumpage Suburbs Supplied Million Gallons	Total Population of Suburbs Served
1957	373,050	4,324,000	58	39,899	760,000
1958	367,269	4,361,000	57	40,298	805,000
1959	377,383	4,393,000	58	43,204	843,000
1960	376,232	4,423,000	58	45,014	873,000
1961	372,173	4,434,000	59	44,646	902,000
1962	383,495	4,463,000	59	46,833	929,000
1963	381,045	4,501,000	61	47,503	965,000
1964	382,717	4,536,000	61	50,241	993,000
1965	361,559	4,592,000	63	50,381	1,041,000
1966	369,137	4,615,000	66	54,182	1,064,000

Source: City of Chicago Water Department. Notice that the increase in population served is caused by an increase in the number of suburbs that buy water from Chicago.

This kind of cooperative venture works. The table doesn't show all the meetings between the Chicago and the suburban officials, the contracts agreed to and written, and the agreements among neighboring suburbs. For example, the village of

Hillside and Berkeley formed a joint water commission which has an agreement with the village of Melrose Park to run a water main through Melrose Park. The water commission also has an agreement with Chicago to buy water for the same rates charged city residents. Chicago pumps its water from Lake Michigan.

Walker Processing Equipment Inc.

Fig. 27

Essential to the growth of a community is pure water in ample supply to meet not only present but future needs. Clarification and softening of the water supply for the residents of Thomasville, Georgia, is accomplished with this unit processing 4,200 gallons per minute.

Other communities near Chicago still use deep wells, instead of buying lake water from the city. This has led to two problems that many smaller towns in growing areas will have to face sooner or later.

First, the well water is harder than the lake water. Home

owners in many communities must have their own water softening equipment. Second, the water table in the wells is dropping. Every few years the pumps in the wells must be set deeper. The water is being used faster than it is flowing into the wells, due to the tremendous growth of population in the area.

The question of whether to use a well, lake or river water might seem unimportant at present in your community. A few years from now, you may realize how important the question was when it was first brought up. Forty years ago, Tulsa officials had the foresight to build a reservoir and a long tunnel extending fifty-five miles to Spavinaw to secure fresh water and end dependence on wells. Perhaps no one knew then that the population of Tulsa would increase from 72,075 in 1920 to 261,685 in 1960 and an estimated 326,500 in 1967. Fortunately, the city did have water for growth.

What are the principal ways to pay for a city water works? There are three methods. Revenue bonds can be sold and the money used to build the system. These bonds are paid only out of the water rates. Or general obligation bonds can be used, pledging tax money for payment. The third possibility, at least for water mains, is special assessment bonds. The bonds are paid by people who pay property taxes on the property along the main. Chapter 11, "Where Does the Money Come From," tells the advantages and techniques of these three kinds of financing.

What was written in Chapter 5 about calling for bids and using the low, reliable bidder for streets applies as well to water works and to all kinds of public works contracts. The contractor is paid periodically for work completed to the date of billing, less a ten per cent reserve, the same as in the case of streets.

Again, careful inspection while water mains are going in must be emphasized. When the main is finished, the engineer tests it with a pressure test. Water pumped in under higher pressure than the maximum load that would be expected tests the main; any weak spot bursts. Final payment isn't made until the water main passes the pressure test.

Good sewers are vital to good health. Dependable sewers protect not only your own city's health but that of towns downstream from you. Everyone is aware that efficient sewage treatment is essential and may even be a life and death matter. Waters polluted by sewage cause serious problems. What most people don't know, however, is that too small a sewage plant can actually halt the growth of a town.

Figure 28 outlines sewage facility construction. If a community, in 1950, had planned a sewage treatment plant twice as large as it needed for its population, the plant would still not be big enough today.

In many cases, health officials have prohibited a city from issuing more building permits until it expanded its sewage treatment plant. Other factors for growth might be near-perfect: buyers who want homes, a new subdivision with an abundance of lots, and a ready builder. If the city's sewage treatment plant wasn't large enough, nothing could grow. In Illinois, officials often have held up or rationed permits in communities with a limited sewage treatment plant.

Fig. 28
VALUE OF INSTALLED CONSTRUCTION
1950-1967

*In millions of dollars

	1950	1955	1960	1963	1964	1965	1966	1967
Sewer systems	383	615	882	947	1,325	1,195	1,300	1,083

Installation of sanitation facilities should keep pace with the projected growth of a community. Recent national figures show less construction despite growing population. Compare this figure with Fig. 4: is your growing community falling behind in the construction of new equipment?

Source: U.S. Bureau of the Census.

To avoid such frustration, plan ahead to make the sewage treatment plant sufficiently large. Meet with officials of neighboring communities and investigate if a joint effort would save everyone money. If there's not enough money without a new bond issue that requires a referendum, have the referendum. Pointers on referendums appear in Chapter 13, "How to Pass a Referendum".

If you've never seen a sewage treatment plant, inspect the various kinds. The simplest type is the oxidation lagoon. This is a pond where the sewage is exposed to the air; that is, oxygen in the air treats the sewage. Sometimes the engineers will install pipes to bubble oxygen through the water. Before you say it must smell terribly, visit one that is managed right and see for yourself. It will smell like fresh water.

For a larger area than can be served by an oxidation lagoon, a sewage treatment plant must be built, one that uses digestors and settling tanks. These are supposed to be odorless, in the sense that there should be no odor detectable outside the grounds. If they operate properly and aren't overloaded, they work that way. These plants discharge their waste into a stream or lake. The discharge water must be kept clean, or the downstream property owners and communities can bring an injunction action in court to stop the pollution.

Pollution from sewage treatment is not inevitable. Recently an overly brave civil engineer, showing off a new treatment plant, scooped up a cup of the treated water flowing out and drank it. You won't have to try such an extreme method. Probably you can find out by questioning the neighbors and the downstream property owners about whether odors emanate from the plant.

During a heavy rainstorm more water can pour into the sewers than the treatment plant can handle. Rain water is supposed to flow into its own storm sewers and not into the sanitary sewers. Some rain water flows into the sanitary sewers in a heavy rain — through leaky joints, basement drains, and illegal connections that admit storm water directly into the sanitary sewer. When too much water pours through the pipes, the treatment plant is unable to handle it. The sewers bypass the treatment plant and the excess flows into the outlet stream or river. The only saving factor is the fact that in a heavy storm, sewage is fairly well diluted by the storm water.

Making the sewers bypass the plant is not the only problem that arises when storm water enters the sanitary sewers. Even a small amount of storm water flowing through the plant reduces its capacity to handle the sanitary sewage it is supposed to. The city may be forced to hold back building permits because of excess storm water.

Walker Processing Equipment Inc.   **Fig. 29**

Property values remain high when local officials are conscientious about providing good services for citizens. North Olmstead, Ohio, modernized its waste water treatment plant with the addition of new equipment.

Deerfield, Illinois, learned how to solve this problem some years ago. In many homes, the village engineer discovered roof drains that were not working correctly. Rain water should have flowed through drainpipes and an underground service line to the front of the lot, and then into a storm sewer main, which led directly to the stream.

In many cases, because of breaks in the hidden underground

pipes caused by ground settling, water from the roof seeped into the sanitary sewers near the house. Water from one roof could add as much load to the sewage treatment plant as water from ten homes. Deerfield officials used a smoke test to discover which homes were emptying storm water into the sanitary sewers. The improvement was dramatic. Almost everyone cooperated willingly, without court action. The village engineer showed them a low cost way using a splash block to divert the water.

Storm water creates a type of problem not often caused by sanitary sewage. Any number of problems can induce citizens to become irritated with their elected officials, but none creates as much annoyance as when a flood during a heavy rainfall ruins furniture and tools stored in basements. When this happens, nothing can really soothe frayed tempers and otherwise ease the situation.

Storm sewer capacity

To reduce the dangers of storm water damage and to increase the effectiveness of the storm sewer systems is a worthy objective. However, the public first must recognize that storm sewers are not designed to be perfect. They may, for example, be designed to handle a five-year storm. This means they will take any amount of water including that from a storm so severe that it occurs only once every five years, on the average. Sometimes the storms are more severe than anticipated, and the water will back into the streets instead of flowing out as fast as it comes down. The cost of preparing for the most severe storms that could conceivably happen is prohibitive. If the city's building regulations miss this fact, there will be trouble.

The building ordinance should require a slope from the house to the street, unless the topographical conditions make it impossible. From time to time, houses are designed with sunken garages with driveways lower than the streets. When the street floods, so does the garage. This could be avoided by planning a slope from the house to the street. Then the home stays dry — even when the street floods. In many cities, a garage below the grade of the ground is prohibited. The city engineer and city attorney can work out an ordinance that will cover conditions in your city.

Second, make the storm sewers more effective by keeping them clean. Dirt washes down from new lawns into the pipes. The mains can break underground, causing parts of the clay-pipe to fall into the joints. In one manhole in a midwestern city, a pair of overalls was fished out. At the first sign that the storm water isn't draining fast enough, send the engineer or inspector to check if the mains need cleaning.

Third, make the storm drains work better by giving the water a place to go. If the water level in the creek is higher than the storm sewer mains that feed into it, the water will stay in the main. Make sure that the creek or river that receives the storm water is kept open.

Filling in land along a creek can reduce the amount of water it can take. This is due to the flood plain. A flood plain is land that usually is not under water, except perhaps a few times a year after heavy rainfall. The fact that the water can flow onto the flood plain keeps the level of the creek much lower than it would be if that water had no place to spread out.

Flood plains

An ordinance regulating the flood plain will help. Most flood plains are private property. For this reason the city can't tell the property owners not to use their land for other purposes. Some effective ordinances specify that the flood plain land cannot be filled in unless an equal amount of flood plain area is provided nearby. This provides the owners with flexibility in planning.

Keeping the creek open is another example of cooperation among various local governments. Where communities are close together, the same creek may meander through several cities or villages. If all think of their neighbors and work out their plans together, they will have better results. Sometimes a separate body politic, such as a drainage district or levee district, will be formed to have jurisdiction over the creeks in several towns. Then the towns can work together and with the drainage district for an overall plan of action.

Calling for bids correctly

Better equipment for the fire department will save the city and its home owners money by reducing their insurance rates. What you want is new equipment without excessive cost. If you call for bids correctly, you can get just that.

A city fire department prepared a call for bids for a new fire truck, stating certain detailed specifications. When the bids came in, only one manufacturer had met the specifications. In fact, because of the way the bids were drawn, only one was able to do so. Obviously, the bid from the manufacturer was high. He knew all the other bids would be rejected.

To understand specifications better, an explanation of how fire trucks are usually made is helpful. The chassis includes the four wheels, motor and cab. The equipment includes everything that goes on that chassis. For a pumper, the equipment will be designed around the pump, with its motor and controls, together with hose. A hook and ladder or a snorkel truck will be designed to hoist the firemen to high places, and may not have a pump on it. In rural areas where there are no hydrants, the fire department will also buy a tank truck to haul water to the fires.

The city can ask for bids separately on the chassis and on the equipment. The specifications need to be written broadly, to describe what performance standards the equipment must meet instead of limiting the bids to one make of equipment. The idea is to give as many bidders as possible a chance, so the bidders will keep the costs down.

Probably financing costs can be saved on a new fire truck by issuing general obligation bonds. The bonds are to be paid out of tax money. This means that you'll get the kind of protection needed, not just the kind that you think you can afford. The suppliers might offer to sell a fire truck on time payment to eliminate the effort of issuing bonds. Check the interest cost. Since bonds are more secure and the interest on the municipal bonds is income tax free, you may find that a lot of interest money can be saved by issuing bonds. If you need a referendum, plan one. Voters generally are for fire protection if the issues are well publicized and the voters are made fully aware of the problem through good public relations work.

No other municipal function has as much impact on land values as a garbage disposal site. An old-fashioned, unsightly dump can drastically reduce the value of nearby land. On the other hand, a well-run disposal site minimizes bad effects, and can eventually increase the land values of the surrounding neighborhood, odd as that may seem.

First, we have to make it clear that there is more than one kind of garbage or refuse, and that there are many kinds of garbage disposal sites or arrangements.

Refuse is a term sometimes used to mean material that has no organic matter in it. That is, it has no food wastes that could create odors, attract vermin and cause disease. Refuse of this kind includes broken concrete, cardboard boxes, metal scraps and papers that are not commercially salvagable.

Refuse might be free of organic matter and still be dangerous to health. Any poisons, dangerous chemicals or paints that are in the material are hazardous. As we'll see later, when we look at the sanitary land fill operation, chemical poisons are a particular threat.

Garbage means waste that includes food wastes and other organic matter. This waste creates the greatest problem. While no completely flawless solution exists, there are several ways of handling it.

Some communities still dispose of garbage and refuse with a

plain, old-fashioned garbage dump. The unsightly dump attracts rats, spreads disease, smells and reduces the value of any property in sight or smelling distance of it.

Many workable alternatives are available. Public officials should refuse to tolerate a plain dump for garbage or refuse. Even though the dump may be used for refuse only, with no food wastes, this uncovered refuse may be a breeding place for rats, and its ugly appearance can do nothing but harm.

Sanitary land fill

Shortly after the end of World War II, the sanitary land fill became a popular substitute for the open dump. A sanitary land fill is placed on low-lying land, in a carefully chosen location.

Trenches are dug in the area to be filled, with the top soil stored in one pile and the clay in another. During the day, trucks dump the refuse into the trench. A heavy tractor drives over the refuse to compress it thoroughly. At the end of each day, clay is dumped into the trench on top of the garbage.

The dig-tamp-fill process continues until the entire land area is filled to the level of the surrounding terrain. Then two feet of clay is placed on the top of the last layer of refuse. Top soil is spread over that. The owner now can plant grass or shrubs on the land. This is how the neighboring land becomes more valuable: instead of a useless low tract, now there is a level, landscaped area. Some land fill operators give the filled-in site to the city or to the park district for a park site. The land is not ideal for building for many years, because it can settle, but it makes a fine playground, baseball diamond or park.

How can a land fill operator afford to give away the filled site? The answer is that it's very profitable to run a land fill near any crowded metropolitan area. Not many places are available for the refuse and garbage. Cities and private scavengers will pay well for the privilege of emptying their trucks anywhere near the area they pick up the refuse and garbage. The shorter the distance their trucks have to go, the less it costs to dispose of the garbage. A private scavenger who owns his own land fill site has a sharp edge in bidding for work, because he can keep down the cost of trucking and the fee for dumping.

City must protect neighbors

No matter how well the land fill is run, it will not be a thing of beauty. Loose papers will blow around. Garbage trucks and the operator's tractor will drive around it. A tall privacy fence will help shield the surrounding property while the land is being filled. City officials can demand this.

If you inspect a few land fill sites in operation, you may notice that the idea of filling to the level of the neighboring land is, in practice, quite flexible. The daily profit of keeping the trucks coming in and paying to unload is high. Some operators prefer to fill in to the level of the top of the nearest hill. At a meeting of a village board in a northern Illinois town, a scavenger even suggested that his land in town would be a great place for developing a ski slope.

If the city officials are alert, arguments can be avoided about how high the land should be filled before the promised park goes in. Before a permit to start the land fill operation is given, demand a site development plan. This plan should show not only what will be on the land, but also the exact elevation of each section when it is finished. Then, a surveyor will be able to determine if the agreement is being fulfilled.

Ask an engineer who understands sanitary land fills for advice on specification for the operation of the land fill. Have your city attorney draw up the necessary ordinances, contracts, and performance bonds to make sure the specifications can be enforced.

If the city public works department rather than a private business firm operates the sanitary land fill, the operation might still be imperfect. The elected public officials must remain alert to the way the work is being done. Without advance notice, drive out and take a look yourself from time to time. Take an engineer along if you want to. You'll soon be able to see how good their housekeeping is. Any little round holes in the ground could be rat holes. Are there papers blowing around? Go back at the end of the day and see if that day's refuse or garbage is out of sight under a clay cover.

Finding space for garbage and refuse

Perhaps the most serious problem for land fills in metropolitan areas is finding space for all the garbage and refuse. Land fill sites are becoming rare and more expensive. Zoning restrictions make it difficult to start a land fill — neighbors will object vigorously to any change in zoning regulations that permits a new site.

Cities and private scavengers continue to explore new ways of disposing of the garbage and refuse without a land fill.

An incinerator reduces the volume of the garbage and refuse to about one-fifth of its former volume. The expense of trucking the ashes to a land fill and the cost of the space needed goes down accordingly. Incinerators pollute the air and a new problem arises. A garbage and refuse incinerator can be designed and operated to keep almost all the harmful ashes, particles and gasses from polluting the air.

Without needing to become an expert on incinerators, a city official should know what to do if his city plans an incinerator or if a private firm asks to operate one. Have an engineer familiar with incinerators prepare specifications both for the construction of the equipment and building and for its safe operation.

Direct the city attorney to prepare an ordinance that will protect the city fully. If the incinerator is to be operated by a private firm, require a bond to guarantee compliance with the anti-pollution regulations.

San Fernando, California, has a new experimental idea for

garbage disposal. A huge revolving drum, with other equipment, aerates the garbage. It requires garbage about six days to move from one end of the drum to the other. The finished product is virtually odorless and can be used as an enricher or fertilizer for gardens and lawns. There may be practical problems associated with this system now, but sooner or later a way will have to be found to convert garbage from its present liability into an asset.

Property values are affected by the way the garbage disposal problem is handled. By using the most efficient method possible for disposal of garbage and refuse, the garbage rates will be kept down. By proper regulation of the disposal site or incinerator, every reasonable effort is exerted to protect the value of nearby land. Firm plans for a park on the land fill site after it is full provide the city with valuable park land at no additional tax cost to the public.

City workers should watch image

Remember, too, that each city employee can do much that is either good or bad for the image of the city. Each garbage collector should know the city policy defining what can be picked up or left. Discuss with garbage collectors the problems of communicating with the public. Be sure they're worthy representatives of city policy.

It's essential that their belief is consistent with city policy. One town's crew, when its truck was mostly empty, would accept furniture that people wished to throw away. They opened a side door to load the items. When the truck was about three-quarters full, they couldn't open the side door and would accept nothing else but garbage. A small matter? The irate citizens felt cheated — they complained that the garbage men took their neighbor's old furniture but not theirs. It would have been much better to have a general clean-up day when everyone could dispose of anything, and to pick up only garbage at other times. This is consistent policy.

The Reading Railroad has a novel idea to discard garbage. It suggests the use of railroad trains to haul garbage to exhausted strip mines in Pennsylvania. Philadelphia is seriously studying the idea. New York City may be interested, too.

Cost control helps homeowners

Cost control of all city public works operations will help reduce the load that homeowners pay to the city. One simple method of cost control is good maintenance of all facilities. A water main that leaks wastes water costs money. There are commercial leak-finding firms that will take a contract to locate all the major leaks in the city.

If you want a rough idea where your city stands, compare the total water pumped as shown on the water works meters with the total amount of water charged to the consumers as indicated on their meters. The total water pumped by the plant will probably be more than the total billed. The difference is being dissipated somewhere — unless unmetered water is being given to some users. Remember, too, that old meters that have never been checked or serviced are probably not registering high enough figures; thus, some users may be paying less than their share.

Sanitary sewer mains will handle more if they are cleaned when they start to clog. If the city hasn't enough sewers to make it worthwhile to buy a machine to clean them, hire a firm to do it. Watch for the industrial wastes that may be interfering with the sewage treatment plant. The city engineer can set up periodic tests of the outflow from any suspected plant. Chapter 16, "Business Regulation Is Important," tells how to induce manufacturers to control their own industrial wastes and limit the load they put on the sewage treatment plant.

Another instance of cooperation with other villages and cities is to buy equipment that avoids duplication. One village may buy sewer rodding machinery; another, a street sweeper; and a third, tree trimming equipment. Agreement ahead of time can be made for rental arrangements so that each municipality will be assured of the use of all three types of equipment and of an income from its own machinery. If there are no legal barriers in your state, it may be possible to loan or rent the crew with the machinery.

Any city official who has to make decisions connected with public works will notice there are numerous experts available to advise him. The problem is to know how to use the experts.

The basic policy decisions about what the city needs to accomplish must be made by the elected officials, not by any of their hired experts. This simple idea is missed too often by many people. The experts tell you how to accomplish the results you want. The city officials must decide what results are needed.

Conflict between city manager and officials

The role of the city manager and that of the elected city officials occasionally result in a raging conflict. As far as the proposal of a new public works project is concerned, the manager is just another city employee. The decision about what new projects are needed is still for the elected officials to make.

Only one question is uppermost when you work with public works proposals; cost estimates, and projections of future needs. What will best protect the health and general welfare of the residents, taxpayers and property owners? A little more money spent on better construction and maintenance will be returned in better living and in dollar savings to the people of your community.

Planners can project how many people and how much industry are likely to inhabit your city ten years from now. An engineer can tell you how much water the estimated future population and industry may use, and what he would do to get the water. The city attorney can explain the ways to finance the cost of the new water works. If your city has a fiscal agent or financial advisor, he'll have some ideas on possible bond issues to pay the cost. But only the elected officials can assemble these elements into a plan that will fit the future of their city.

8

Libraries are for people

--not books

LIBRARIES HAVE THREE explosions to face. The population explosion means they must serve more people. The information explosion means people demand more books, periodicals, newspapers and reports of all kinds. Finally, the libraries have created their own explosion: a rapid expansion of the kinds of services a library can give.

The purpose of a library is to serve people. Some libraries lack the proper attitude of helpfulness, and as a public official or interested citizen, you should investigate how yours is performing.

Talking to children who use the library is a practical way to evaluate the library's attitude. In a new Illinois library, seventh graders were working on a school assignment in the section where senior high school and adult books are stored. After a few minutes, an assistant librarian approached them indignantly and said, "You're in the wrong section! You disturb everyone." Fortunately, this type of library attitude which protects books from public use is rare. It should be.

If you wonder if you have a library in the best sense of the word or merely a mausoleum for books, observe the attitude of the library personnel. Some libraries have carefully instructed their personnel to make the public feel it is always welcome. Others are places of gloom — more because of the personnel's attitude than the effect of an old building or a physical facility.

A library should be cheerful

Officials in charge of the library should demand that a cheerful atmosphere prevails. In most states there is a separate board of library trustees to administer local library affairs. Usually the library trustees are responsible to the city council or commission, and must seek their tax support from the city council members who are willing to appropriate and levy taxes for this purpose. In a few instances, the library trustees have authority to levy their own taxes, are elected directly by the voters and are accountable only to the voters. More typically, library trustees are responsible to the city fathers, and are appointed by them. State laws in some states permit a number of variations. The board of library trustees might have only one library building or a dozen spread throughout an entire county.

Regardless of the variations, all library trustees have one thing in common: They are responsible only for library services. They can devote themselves wholly to this aspect of public service. Although many library trustees work full time in the business world, they make sure that the personnel of the library perform as they are directed to.

Directly under the library trustees is the librarian. Technically there is only one librarian; the others whom we usually call librarians are assistant librarians or clerks. In most fair-sized communities, the librarian holds a Master's degree in library science.

The trustees can look to the librarian to set standards for the assistant librarians and all other employees. Ordinarily the trustees shouldn't give orders or register complaints directly to employees. The librarian should know what the trustees want, and supervise the employees accordingly.

A good librarian needs three qualities

Three attributes for a successful librarian are: (1) she should be basically friendly and optimistic; (2) she needs specialized education so that she can be helpful in assisting those who use the library, and (3) she should be well-groomed. These same attributes are what the librarian in turn should demand from those she employs. Of course, men also are capable as librarians and in other library positions.

For a number of years, libraries like the ones in Chicago and Oak Park, Illinois, have had music centers where people can listen to, or borrow records. Not everyone has had an opportunity to hear good music at home, or anywhere else, except at the library. Here's a way to introduce people to a pleasant experience. Most people who know and enjoy good music can't afford to buy all the records they want. The library is the only agency that can provide this needed service.

The music department of the library isn't in competition with the music stores. It keeps the people who are not ready to buy away from the stores. It can interest more people in good music, and thus creates potential customers for music stores.

The Tulsa Public Library's art department provides two services. First, reproductions of art works may be borrowed. Second, the original works of local artists on display may be rented or purchased. The rental is low. This gives the work of local artists some exposure, and a chance to make sales.

Many libraries have scheduled summer story hour programs. These benefit young children by exposing them to the fun of books and the joy of visiting the library. Naturally, it's important to have a calm, self-assured person to take charge of the story hour.

Tulsa's library has an experimental lunch meeting. A film or lecture is presented while the audience eats box lunches.

Either as a library trustee, or as a person interested in library affairs, you have an extra asset to help you discover how to develop a better library. The librarian is trained and experienced to assist with your research. How many other department heads in local government are so well equipped?

Some librarians and library trustees have gone beyond the research stage. They have instituted short courses for new library trustees.

The newly-appointed trustee meets with the librarian, the president of the library board and as many library trustees as can get together at the same time. The president presents a prepared outline of library services and duties of the library trustees. The broad scope of library activities, including books, music, art, story hours, lectures, and movies should be explained. The methods of raising money should also be outlined. Most libraries receive some real estate tax money and some voluntary contributions.

Ways to help the library

Friends of the library may contribute money as well as time and effort. The scope of the authority of the trustees must be covered also.

It's part of the duty of the president of the library board (not the librarian) to explain to the new trustee the differing spheres of the librarian and the library trustees. The assistant librarians, clerks and other employees report to the librarian, not to the trustees. The trustees act officially only in their meetings. If the trustees want the librarian to change anything, a vote of the trustee at a meeting is the method to be used.

The flood of new books strains the efforts of the librarian and trustees to keep pace. They must find new ways to disseminate information. One simple, effective way to get more books in use is to have more books in circulation. This also reduces the number of books in the library. Books are circulated by advertising, by being courteous, by preparing and publishing information about books, by forming discussion interest groups, by having library branches, by using bookmobiles, and by getting people into the libraries by every means short of kidnapping.

Fig. 30

An attractive public library, such as this one at Orchard Lake, Michigan, which won an award of merit for design, invites the public to use its books. A town's cultural aspirations are reflected by how well its library system is organized and operated.

The books must be managed along with all the other library clerical work. Question the cherished customs and determine if old methods can be improved. Use imagination and attempt innovations. A library should be willing to try better ways to circulate books.

Is everything your library does necessary? How about collecting fines? Are they worth it? If the board of library trustees approves of the idea, collecting fines could be eliminated. Some libraries have done it, with few ill effects. It was found that the library staff was spending too much time figuring fines and making change. Now these employees are doing something more productive with their time. Do fines deter people from bringing books in late? Ask the girl who collects them. Ask how many people who bring in books late are repeaters. If the fines worked, the same people wouldn't be late again and again. If the minutes required to collect fines amount to an hour a day, that's hundreds of extra hours wasted each year — hours that could be used to make your library more attractive and efficient.

Check the duties that each employee has. The librarian must make certain decisions that can't be delegated. An efficient librarian can train most assistants for tasks such as marking Dewey Decimal System numbers on new books. Assistants can send old books to the librarian for a decision on whether to reshelve or to dispose of them. When a book crosses an assistant's desk, he should ask himself, "Does this book belong on the shelf or should I ask the librarian to remove it?" At least once a year, assistants should go through all the books and list those which are no longer useful. The librarian can decide which to keep or discard.

About twenty years ago, libraries began saving space by microfilming material. Now many libraries have at least some microfilm. Newspapers often are microfilmed; this saves storage space and keeps news items and legal notices available indefinitely.

Although libraries haven't much need for computers to store information as yet, they are using a few in specialized ways. Tulsa, for example, puts its catalog through computers rather than on cards. The computer prints the information on a few volumes of books and keeps it up-to-date. A shelf of books several feet long will replace a card catalog the size of an average kitchen.

When a reader wants to find a book by author, title or

subject, he looks through the catalog volume instead of rows of cards in the old card catalog. More than space is saved. It saves the time of the reader. In larger cities, he doesn't have to go to the main library to see what books it has. The computer furnishes identical volumes for each branch library, and can do the same for each bookmobile. A reader who is unable to visit the main library can conduct any research job at a branch. He orders the book he needs from the main library after locating it in the book catalog.

This set of catalog volumes printed by the computer reveals at which branch library each book is located.

Computerized research

The next step will be toward computerized research. If a code number is fed into the computer, it sends back all the information stored on a particular subject. Far-fetched? It's already under study for law libraries. The World Peace Through Law Center, with headquarters in Geneva, Switzerland, is studying a computer to store all international law decisions in its memory banks.

Statutes, treaties and international court decisions would be fed into the memory bank of the computer. For example, a lawyer who wants to know the law on restraints on oil shipments to certain countries, can feed the question into the computer and find all the official action on that point. The computer will not answer a specific question of law any more than any book can. It merely prints information on comparable cases.

Such computerized research could be designed for any subject, not just law. Perhaps this will be one of the wonders of the future. A library user will look at an index for a code number, put the code number into the computer, and it will tell him instantly how to build a barbecue pit.

Some universities are working on a plan for computerized memory storage for all kinds of information. A group called

Educom was formed to look into the technological, indexing and copyright problems. There were eight in the group when it started; now there are 87.

There is a simple way, requiring no complicated gadgets, for your library to expand its services tremendously: cooperate with other libraries. The high school, college and county courthouse law libraries in your neighborhood may enter into a mutual assistance pact. Public libraries in adjacent cities or library districts may also be willing to join such an agreement.

Without losing local control over your library, ways can be worked out to improve service to the public with such cooperation.

First, agree that any of your borrowers can use a book from the other cooperating libraries. The book can be sent to your library, or if the reader prefers, he can visit the cooperating library himself and use or take out the book just as he would locally.

While trading books doesn't take any more gadgetry than a telephone, a computer would make it work even better. If the library's catalog is on the computer, the computer can print the catalog in book form. It would be easy to make an extra set of books for each cooperating library.

Independent library systems cooperate

Second, several small, independent library systems can cooperate in buying books and often receive a substantial volume discount. Select one librarian as the central purchasing agent. Each independent city or village library would keep the decision-making power on what books it would buy. The central purchasing office would merely send for the books each local library orders.

The Oak Park librarian tried this system for several years, and reports that it is working well.

There is one task that a local public library can do probably better than any other agency, and that is to set aside space for local history material. Many years ago, a young lawyer in Illinois helped a group of citizens form a new city. They were either grateful or unable to pay his fee, so they named the city after him. Imagine the value of a historical document or newspaper item which relates the establishment of Lincoln, Illinois, by Abraham Lincoln.

Somewhere in your city there is a person who may be famous someday. What information you have in your local history section will help his biographers years from now, and prove your foresight.

Be selective about news clippings

The trick is to be selective — not every scrap of news about everyone in a town can be saved. Someone who may become famous sooner or later will do enough to get into your files. One system is to save an annual church bulletin. Certain editions should carry a list of church officers. A church program for a church anniversary celebration rates a place in the files.

When a new business is opened, there may be a printed program or news releases telling about it. Save it. Abraham Lincoln and Harry S Truman were businessmen, of sorts, in their day. You don't need every special sale ad, but wouldn't it be exciting to own a bulletin of the opening of Truman's haberdashery? Even if none of your merchants goes into politics, one of them may grow into a big enough businessman to be an interesting subject for study. Anyone who has lived in your town for a few years will enjoy going back in time to read historical materials. Most of these documents are gone forever if the local library doesn't save them. If you're the nervous type, make photocopies for public use and lock up the originals.

Probably you'll have all the local newspapers on microfilm. Even so, there are occasional items of such obvious historic value that they should be clipped and organized into notebooks. The opening of the new library, the completion of the freeway and the building of the city hall are important enough to warrant special filing.

To make a selection, ask yourself, will someone want to see this in ten or twenty years?

Fig. 31

American Library Association

A branch library reaches out to the people, and should exemplify the spirit and service of the entire system. This one does. The Sequoyah Hills branch of the Knoxville library system is spacious, generously lighted, and well-stocked with books. Its design won an award of merit.

Encourage local photographers to donate occasional pictures. Diaries or travel memoirs are difficult to find, therefore keep any you get. Let the public know what you collect and you'll probably receive similar contributions.

The public library doesn't need to keep government records. These will be kept at the village hall or city hall, the county building, or with the various clerks or secretaries charged by law with keeping them. An informed librarian will know where the local government archives are kept, and can direct a reader to the right source for the information he wants.

While all the historical data of the city could be put on microfilm, it will be more valuable in its original form.

Some librarians and library trustees do research in color psychology. The library's decor makes you feel like staying and reading. In general, soft yellows and beiges are favored for background color of the walls. A livelier color, such as an intense red or blue, will make the chairs look inviting, and induce readers to sit and relax. Color can enliven older library buildings that have seen better days.

Your city may need a new library building. It seems that most of the library buildings in the United States are either brand new or over forty years old. This isn't just an accident. So many library buildings were built with Carnegie funds generations ago that for a long time very few sensed the need for newer buildings.

How to raise money for the library

For the needed funds to build a new library, you'll need a bond issue. In most states, you must have a referendum before you can sell bonds.

You will not sell bonds for the library or for any other purpose unless you go about it carefully. The chapter on "How to Sell a Referendum" gives details on how the Tulsa library board at first lost a referendum. Later, with virtually the same voters, the library board passed the referendum. Things must have been done right the second time.

Preparation for a possible referendum goes on all the time. The manner in which the public is treated at the library, the library's news releases and bulletins, the new ways the library finds to serve the community — all will help decide the outcome of a bond issue election.

To help in the referendum, and as a matter of intelligent planning, a new building program must be designed to serve the entire village or city. If the village is so small that you can get a site within bicycling distance of any home, one building may be enough. For a smaller town, one building is the most efficient. The staff can be smaller and it'll be simpler to keep track of the books. The cost of building construction will be less, too. Building maintenance, of course, will be more economical.

Needs according to size

A larger community has greater needs. If people who don't drive can't reach a neighborhood library easily, the library board is not serving their interests. Choose building sites throughout the area you serve. For a library board serving an entire county, this will mean many branch libraries.

If some sparsely-settled farm areas are included in the library district, you won't be able to have a library within strolling distance of each farm house. You can build a library close to where almost everyone gathers, though. There are areas in nearby towns where people congregate, such as shopping districts, movies, busy intersections and town squares. Choose strategic locations convenient for people to reach.

Consider, too, that people no longer go to the library by horse and buggy. Find a location that offers ample off-street parking. Even in small towns with no parking problems, a special lot for library parking is inviting. In a congested area the library may need meters or a stamp system to discourage shoppers who seek free parking.

Figure 32 shows how the Tulsa City-County Library System located its libraries in strategic spots throughout the county. Each separate municipality has its own branch library. The committee doing the planning also brought the number of branch libraries in outlying areas within the county of Tulsa up to a total of about twenty. A book may be borrowed from the main library as well as from any branch.

What kind of a building do you need to house the complete

library services the community needs? Perhaps a better question would be, what kind of a building will you need in ten or fifteen years?

Populations are increasing. The amount and type of library service expected by the population is also increasing, and these will keep on growing as the public learns more about library services.

On the other hand, the reality that you have only so much tax money available must be faced when you design the building for the future. Voters may hesitate to vote for a structure much larger than is immediately necessary. The building committee and the architect must plan realistically for the present with current resources.

Fig. 32

HOW TULSA SPREAD LIBRARY SERVICES
THROUGHOUT AN ENTIRE COUNTY

Facility	No. of Locations
Main library	1
Branches in the city	11
Branches in neighboring towns	8
Regular bookmobile services to schools and communities	25
Total places to get books	45

These 45 locations are in addition to cooperating university, county and law school libraries.

Source: Tulsa City-County Library System Reports.

The answer, then, seems to be insistence on an expandable building design. The branch library in an area where land costs are not too high might be designed as a one-story plant, with possible expansion by adding a new wing. In the downtown district where land costs might be prohibitive, the committee ought to look into a building several stories high, with a structure strong enough to sustain several more stories. In the Tulsa City-County Library, if you walk up the back stairs to the top floor, you'll notice stairs going up to the ceiling ready for the next floor when the library needs it.

Using library space effectively

While there are some very experienced architects designing public buildings, there is the problem of understanding how people will use the space for various special functions. The building committee of the library can't expect the architect to know just what it needs unless it is very specific, and insistent, about the special needs of the public while it is at the library and how much space each activity takes.

If you will have a lecture room, how many people will be present at the most popular meetings? Have you provided for elbow and leg room? Do you need wide aisles so that people can stand around and discuss issues after the lecture? Will the room be used for productions that need a stage?

Regardless of the stature of the architect, the building committee and the board of trustees of the library must make these decisions. The architect will gladly furnish rough cost estimates, and advise on the latest kinds of furniture available. For example, there are colorful, easily cleaned plastic chairs that can interlock into rows or be taken apart and rearranged in different ways. The lecture room can be more flexible if the seats aren't fixed.

Designing reading rooms

Design the reading rooms for comfortable reading. Have plenty of space for table and chair groups, as well as upholstered chairs or couches. The readers are your "customers." If you help them enjoy their reading, they'll be back. Figure 33 shows a typical layout of a part of a reading room.

Keep the readers in mind when you design the stacks, and

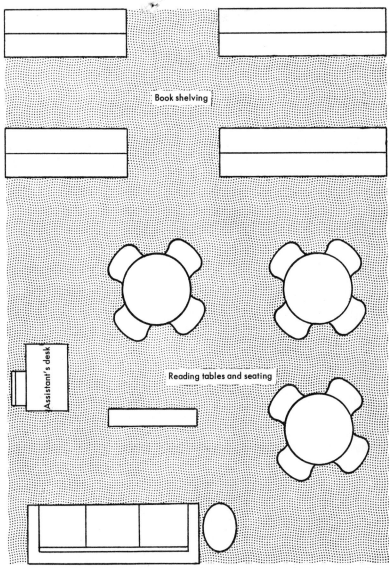

Fig. 33
READING ROOM LAYOUT

Book shelving

Reading tables and seating

Assistant's desk

The reading room layout should encourage people to stay and browse.

plan the number of square feet you need for the books you plan to have. Stacks about five feet high are more inviting than stacks that reach to the ceiling. Besides, if you start with low stacks, you'll have some room to expand later without adding on to the building.

Innovations in library use

The next innovation about library building may surprise you. The library at the main campus at Northwestern University has facilities for those who want to use typewriters.

Why not? If your library has any kind of a book collection at all, it will attract students and hopeful writers. If you've an impressive local history section, you may attract biographers, historians and novelists who seek authentic local color. If the people served by the library can benefit from a sound-absorbent typing room, plan for one.

Perhaps even more modern are the little booths and cubby-holes that a few libraries have for those who want to use a tape recorder.

Somewhere in the floor plan, easily accessible to the public, there should be an area for the machines that the readers need. A self-service copying machine requires convenient floor space. Microfilm readers should be near where the microfilm files are.

Make sure you allow desk space for the assistant librarians.

In the music section, plan enough space to store the records and tapes next to the turntables and tape players. If you haven't space for separate listening booths, plan to install earphones.

For paintings, you need several kinds of space. A few easels and bulletin boards can display the works you think deserve attention. Wall space will help. Next, a rack with sliding storage spaces would be desirable. A separate desk for checking out paintings might help.

What was said earlier in this chapter about the color psychology of a building applies even more to a new building's interior than to renovating an old one. With a new structure, work with more than color. Texture for interest could include some rough stucco, wood paneling and window walls with drapes or vertical blinds. If you're planning picture windows, make sure they have an interesting view.

When you're in a quandary about library planning, think of the basic rule: Libraries are for people, not for books.

9

No one is against

better schools

SCHOOL BOARD OFFICIALS and citizens who are interested in the public schools are being buffeted by the winds of change. Shortages of teachers, insufficient schools, conflicting theories of integration, decisions that put new definitions on what is illegal, and dissident education theories — each pushes the school board in a different direction. At the same time, teachers, administrators and parents sometimes become locked in a power struggle.

Life is trying enough without such controversies. The pressure of growing school age populations and towns outgrowing their existing schools are enough. Figure 34 shows how rapidly school age population has been shooting up since 1940, compared to the number of teachers. These are averages;

growing school districts in towns that had a building boom had a much faster growth.

In a town that has new homes the problem often is severe. There's a tax gap: it takes from one to several years before the tax money for a new home starts to come in to the school district. Meanwhile the school board has to pay several hundred dollars a year to educate each child in that new home, and also meet the cost of the added building space that is needed. Multiply this situation by the hundred or so homes in each new subdivision. Two or three rapidly-built subdivisions can throw the school board a million dollars off schedule.

On a more encouraging vein, at the same time, we've seen exciting changes in education in the past generation. The teaching of mathematics has been up-dated, to the mystification of some parents. Students at young ages are being encouraged to try more sophisticated science projects. These are only the beginnings of change.

Foreign languages are being taught in some schools so the students converse in the language, not just talk about it. With the new emphasis on conversation and pronunciation before the study of reading, spelling, and grammar, foreign language teaching has been greatly improved. The use of conversational records and tapes made by natives in the language also helps.

Fig. 34

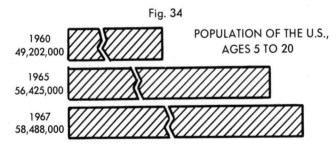

1960 49,202,000	POPULATION OF THE U.S., AGES 5 TO 20
1965 56,425,000	
1967 58,488,000	

This is the total population, not the total enrolled in schools. That is, the population the schools should be serving, not the population actually served. In 1966 there were 48,988,000 elementary and secondary school pupils (including kindergarten).

Source: U.S. Bureau of the Census.

Teaching machines will become more popular. Properly used, they help all students learn faster, and some students learn much faster. They supplement, but can never replace, the teachers.

Money will have to be found to employ trained personnel and buy needed equipment to keep your school district up-to-date.

School board challenges

Many challenges face the school boards. They can meet them all. There's a story about an old bookkeeper who always knew the right way to answer a question. Every morning when he arrived for work, he unlocked his desk drawer, peered at a note hidden in it, closed the drawer and went to work. Afterwards no problem or complication could stump him. His fellow workers wondered what was written on the note.

Upon his retirement, the old gentleman bequeathed his desk to his chief assistant. The assistant arrived early the next day. Hurrying to the desk, he feverishly unlocked the drawer, pulled it open, and looked at the note. It read, "The debits go on the left side".

There is also an answer to all the school problems that keep arising. Take a piece of paper and put it in your desk drawer. On it write, "The purpose of schools is to educate children".

A generation ago we wouldn't have needed this fundamental statement. Now, amid the confusion in the field of education, there is no useful way to discuss schools without starting with this basic principle.

Actually, there are numerous proved ideas available now to help your school system educate children. The problem is to implement the ideas so that they do what they are designed to do.

For example, teachers' aids can contribute to educating children by helping to overcome the teacher shortage. A teacher spends up to one-third of her time on unproductive

SUPER JU JITSU COURSE: Hall, Nelson. Big illustrated home-study course on the art and science of practicing and using this method of applying Lightning-Quick American Super Ju Jitsu. The weapons are just the bare hands. (76 lessons in six units, paper.)
Cat. No. 38   Postpaid, only $11.95

SHOE REPAIRING COURSE: Sarlette, Ralph. Practical, well-illustrated, step-by-step series of lessons on how to repair and rebuild shoes. Written for the beginner who wants to go into business or the family man who wants to save money by doing his own shoe repairing.
Cat. No. 44   Postpaid, only $7.95

'POPULATION CONTROL' THROUGH NUCLEAR POLLUTION: Tamplin, A. R. and Gofman, J. W. These famous scientists contend that the present allowable radiation dosage from "peaceful atoms" will result· in 32,000 deaths each year from cancer and leukemia. Attacking the AEC, they demand that the use of atomic energy to operate power plants or to blast caves for natural gas storage be suspended until adequate safety devices against atomic waste and leaks are perfected. Provocative and controversial.
Cat. No. 10   Postpaid, only $6.95

COMPLETE COURSE IN PROFESSIONAL PIANO TUNING, REPAIR, AND REBUILDING: Stevens, Floyd A. Teaches how to tune pianos like a craftsman. Fully illustrated lessons easily mastered by a beginner. Covers repair and tuning of all piano styles. Reveals many trade secrets. Includes electronic organ and piano tuning. Tells how to start a business. Author is a Ph.D., musician, guild instructor and craftsman.
Cat. No. 7   Postpaid, only $19.95 (s)

COMPLETE COURSE IN PROFESSIONAL LOCKSMITHING: Robinson, Robert L. A home study course in one volume—at a fraction of the cost. Easy-to-master instruction; over 200 photos and diagrams. How to repair, service, replace, alter and rebuild all types of locks. Includes lock picking, decoding, masterkeying, electronic lock repairs; how to start a lock repair shop.
Cat. No. 15   Postpaid, only $29.95 (s)

CONVERSATION TODAY: Dahlquist, Albert. An interesting self-instruction course, in one volume, on the practical techniques of influencing people with the voice. Shows how to win friends, inspire respect, gain business cooperation and advancement, get people to do what you want them to do.
Cat. No. 66   Postpaid, only $7.95

HANDWRITING ANALYSIS: Bunker, M. N. The art and science of understanding human behavior by Graphoanalysis. The largest, most authoritative treatment of personality assessment through scientific handwriting analysis. Written by the founder of the International Graphoanalysis Society. Contains a wealth of illustrations.
Cat. No. 68   Postpaid, only $6.95

PSYCHO-SALES-ANALYSIS: Huttig, Jack A widely-known sales executive teaches you how to sharpen your selling skills to sell products, services, and especially yourself. Unique self-analysis exams before and after each chapter insure mastery of subject matter. Chapters on developing prospects, creating desire, improving personality, etc. Instructive, fascinating and yet easy to read.
Cat. No. 9   Postpaid, only $9.9

RELEASE FROM ISOLATION: How t Find Friendship, Love, and Happiness Martindale, J. S. A psychologist explain how to escape isolation and find ident and a place in life by forming small, natu gestalt groups. A guide to living.
Cat. No. 8   Postpaid, only $7.

TRIANGLE: The Betrayed Wife: Berg Evelyn Miller. How a wife may cope w anger, despair and frustration when s finds her husband is unfaithful. A no psychologist offers wise advice on how save a marriage. Absorbing case histori
Cat. No. 13   Postpaid, only $7

'I HAD THE CRAZIEST DREAM LA NIGHT': Steele, Marion A. and Armstro Ronald M. Dreams try to tell you ab your worries, wishes and conflicts. Steele, a psychiatrist, explains how to meaning out of good, bad, and sex drea
Cat. No. 16   Postpaid, only $6

details: filling out attendance records, taking up collections, completing forms and making announcements that use up time which should be devoted to instruction or class discussion. A teacher's aid could record the attendance unobtrusively by looking over the seating chart to see who is present without interrupting the class session. This means that not only the teacher's time, but the entire class's time is saved. The teacher's aid might grade some papers. In the matter of grading written stories or essays, the teacher's training and experience is necessary. However, the aid can check sentence completion, true-or-false, and multiple-choice tests.

Misuse of teachers' aids

That is what teachers' aids are supposed to do, not what they really do. Usually the teacher's aid is put to work cranking out mimographed material or doing clerical tasks in the principal's office. There is no measurable benefit to the education of the children from the customary misuse of teachers' aids.

When the teachers' aids system is used well, the teacher is free to give individual instruction to her students. If your school system has a teachers' aids program, investigate what the teachers' aids really do.

How much more time does the teacher have because of the teacher's aid? Go, without an appointment, and see for yourself. No amount of reading about it or asking others will do.

Once in a while the school district may try to save teachers' time by having volunteer parents grade school compositions. This idea doesn't seem too promising. It will save the teachers some time, but it doesn't educate children when untrained people comment and grade their compositions. The purpose of reading a composition is to discover how to help the student write better. Such comment must be on a level of development that is suitable for the age intended. The teacher can make notes on the paper and talk to the student to bring out his strong points and overcome his weak points. She must use judgment to improve each student without overwhelming him. She can also deduce from the written compositions what type of errors her class is making and teach to meet specific needs.

Teacher recruiting program

The only way to have enough teachers is to create a sound recruiting program. Lombard forms a parents' committee to interview prospective new teachers. The committee members study the school system in order that they can talk intelligently about tenure, salaries, benefits and retirement plans. The prospective teachers ask for information on working conditions, buildings and equipment. Severe discipline problems in some schools will discourage many teachers.

If your community appoints a recruiting committee made up of parents, help your committee members to do an effective job. The competition for teachers is intense. The teachers can go anywhere in the state, once they are licensed there. They can often go to another state and qualify. Competing for you are all the school districts in the fifty states.

Teachers are the most important part of the educational picture. As you read this chapter on all the aspects of the school system and school problems, keep in mind how every question and decision will affect teacher recruiting.

Salaries are not the only factor teachers consider when they look for a job — but pay is one area where you'll have to meet your competition if you want the pick of the better candidates. We hear arguments on how teachers are well-paid for the hours they put in, as well as discussion on how poorly-paid they think they are. All this conversation is irrelevant. The point is that to employ qualified teachers, you must pay good salaries.

If your district doesn't have enough money to meet competitive salaries, you'll have to raise funds somehow. In some states, school districts can have a referendum to raise the maximum tax rate and raise salaries. Chapter 13, "How to Pass a Referendum," explains how to enhance the chance to win.

Fig. 35

ation's Schools

Much of today's more attractive architecture is reflected by new schools. The Bunyan Elementary School in Newbury Park, California, is spacious and fitting for the sunny climate and dry terrain. Note the wide verandah and handsome court.

Schools at least have one aid to pass a referendum. The National Congress of Parents and Teachers can offer help to get out a favorable vote. Chapter 13 tells how to use volunteer help to set up a "telephone tree," keep track of those who voted, and provide transportation and a baby-sitting service for voters. The PTA doesn't need to wait for volunteers. The officers can appoint people to work.

In other states, the state legislature can authorize more funds and higher salaries. Compare your state with other states and see if you need to go to your legislature.

The fast growth of the school age population has given every school board problems relating to the building of new structures. When your district needs a new school, you will need the support of the public to pass a referendum for a bond issue. There is no magic way to win public support. The school board has to prove that it is working for the best interests of education. If voters think the board is not being honest with the public, if costs are being hidden or misrepresented, or if the costs of floating the bond issue are carelessly handled, voters justifiably will be suspicious.

Once in a while a school board will decide to have a building bond issue without assigning a lawyer to represent its interests. However, experienced public officials rely on a lawyer. This is important in dollars and cents. A slight advantage in the interest rates can save the school district thousands of dollars over the life of the bonds.

The school district's own attorney can give the school board the edge it needs to get the lowest possible interest rate.

If you have a referendum to erect a new school to serve just a new part of town, people in the old part might wonder why they should support a school their area doesn't need. The answer is that overcrowding anywhere will harm the entire system. If there is increasing population in one part of town and no new school to serve the children, the children will have to be sent to the older schools. If this overcrowds the old schools, you will need split shifts to teach the overflow.

In view of the trend of Supreme Court decisions on the right of all students to equal schooling, the district must provide adequate classroom space throughout the district, or bus students around to reduce overcrowding. There is no reason for parents in one section of the district to feel that overcrowding in another area is not their problem.

Before you start to work on the referendum, you'll have to decide how to spend the money. The people selecting the site will have estimates of future numbers of school children in various subdivisions. Builders and subdividers can give estimates. Children in school fill out forms telling how many pre-school brothers and sisters they have.

Fig. 36

Tasteful design is combined with function and convenience for special students in this harmonious structure. The J.P. Widney High School for the handicapped in Los Angeles is representative of California's concern for its citizens.

First, with the help of the superintendent, the administrative staff and whatever planners you have, you will decide whether you need a new school or a new wing on an existing school.

Fig. 37

Nation's Schools

A school district looks ahead. The library of Orland Park (Illinois) Jr. High School is large and ready for an expanding student body. Note the abundance of lighting.

If you must build a new school, you will need a firm written contract to buy the land before you start the referendum. Find land not only accessible to many students, but also useful from other standpoints. Can enough extra land be bought to provide for playground space, parking space, and space for future building and expansion? Look for land near a park so that the park school plan may be more easily worked out. Talk to the park board and learn what their land acquisition plans are. You may be able to tie the two together.

., After selecting the land, instruct the school district attorney to work out a binding contract. In most states, the contract can state that it is contingent on the passage of the school bond issue referendum. Your attorney may require a down payment to make the contract binding.

In some cases you may need an option rather than a contract. For an option, you must pay the owner some money, which he can keep whether the referendum passes or not. The contract or option must be negotiated between the land owner and the school district. You don't have to call for bids to buy land. Most public officials get at least two appraisals as a basis for making an offer for land.

Condemnation suits

If the landowner won't sell, or if he wants more than the school board wants to pay, you can still acquire the land. Have your attorney file a condemnation case. In some states appraisers are appointed by the court, and in other cases the jury hears only appraisers representing the property owners and the school district. In any event, the jury verdict determines what the land is worth. The jury does not decide whether the school board ought to buy the land, but only the value.

After the referendum comes the important step of spending the money. First, the school board pays for the land, and secures a deed. Next, it must begin planning for constructing.

The architect had to have at least preliminary plans and an estimate of costs before the referendum. After the referendum, the architect puts the plans and specifications in final form, ready for construction, so that contractors can make bids.

The school board does not ask for bids for the architect's services. The reason is that these are professional services on which the board relies because of the special competence of the man they hire. Some public officials choose to use a structural engineer as well as an architect.

The question that will come up at this point is how the new school will look. Some voters think that cost-conscious architecture has to look drab. An imaginative architect can design a pleasant, cheerful, colorful building for about the same price as a building that looks like a barracks. Make sure the voters know that individuality is not expensive.

Fig. 38

The most valuable asset that a community can have is plenty of land on which to build schools. Such needs must be anticipated years ahead. The Homestead Elementary School of Bel Aire, Maryland, not only has a lovely, natural playground, but ample room for adding new buildings if needed.

The way the school board calls for bids on new construction of a new building or an addition to an old structure can save or waste money. The main object of calling for bids is not to go through a ceremony, but to make sure that you get the lowest possible price from a competent firm. Allow plenty of time, not just the minimum that the law requires. The contractors will want to contact subcontractors before they bid. Send copies of the call for bids to anyone you think is qualified. The architect and the structural engineer will have names of possible bidders. You can charge for copies of plans that builders take out. Many public officials make the deposit refundable if the contractor brings in a bid.

A school board that has a reputation for honesty and integrity will get the best bids time after time. If a bid is rejected on a flimsy technicality in order to give the job to someone who bid higher, reputable contractors will not be eager to bid low on the next job. Since the purpose of taking bids is to insure the best price for the public, don't throw out a bid on a technicality. Give the bidder a chance to correct his error.

Fig. 39

IBM

A progressive school system welcomes new ideas, even mechanical aids. Teaching machines help reduce the work load of teachers. Depending on the type of the device, machines may also speed the learning process.

School building contracts, like most public works contracts, usually provide for part payment as the work goes along. The architect will certify the value of what has been done to date, withhold the amount of reserve set by the contract, and show the net amount due. Most contracts prefer to withhold ten per cent of the amount due until final completion. When all the work is finished and accepted, the school board approves payment of the balance, including the ten per cent reserve, to the contractor.

Keeping up with subdivisions

Fast-growing school districts have had to be resourceful to keep up with the growing subdivisions. This is particularly true in a district where homes are in a price class and location that attracts couples with school-age children. In one summer, enough children to fill a school can come into an area that was formerly farmland. It takes more than one summer to prepare a bond issue, have a referendum, sell bonds, call for building bids, erect a school building, and equip it for occupancy.

To make matters more complicated, the real estate taxes on the new houses are not collected and turned over to the school board right away. Typically, the school district will educate the children in the new subdivision for at least a year before the school district receives tax money from the new homes.

There are two things that the school district must do to protect itself. This is an area where cooperation with other local bodies, the land developers and builders, and the public is essential.

The Elgin, Illinois, school district showed the way to provide first aid to overcrowded schools, through cooperation. A group of angry parents met in a town near Elgin to decide what to do about the absence of a school in their neighborhood. Their children were transported several miles by bus. Split shifts were threatened.

Instead of painting picket signs and marching against the

school board and the subdivision builder, the parents determined to find a way to solve the problem. They consulted a lawyer. They investigated what minimum requirements would be for temporary classroom space. Next, they contacted a builder to learn if he could offer temporary space. The builder had some model homes that the school district could use. He asked for enough rent to pay interest on the loans covering the buildings. The school board accepted his offer. This gave the neighborhood children classroom space in their own neighborhood for a year. Meanwhile, work was started on financing a new school.

This was a voluntary arrangement. Some school boards, with the help of city officials, have abused the idea of voluntary payments by builders. They have forced builders to pay money to the school districts to help with educational costs. The technique is for the city to refuse to approve some part of the builder's project until a so-called voluntary payment is made to the school board. This coercion is illegal and unnecessary.

Plan for industry

There is an effective way for the city officials to help the school district's tax picture. Plan for more industry. Improve the facilities to serve and attract industry. Zone land suitable for this purpose. These steps will add to the taxable value of the real estate in the school district, without adding to the number of children. Similarly, commercial development will help the school board's tax problem.

The school board can stretch its land acquisition funds and building money by using the park-school plan.

The park-school plan is described in detail in Chapter 2, "The Revolution in Park Land Management." The school board and the park board arrange to buy adjacent land. The park board furnishes the playground and the school furnishes the school building. There are many possible· variations: the park board's field house can be used for school sports, and school rooms can be used after hours for the park board's recreation activities.

The Chicago school board tried to solve some of its overcrowding problems by using mobile classrooms, which are mounted on wheels like trailers. This idea had some unfortunate effects. It resulted in keeping Negro children in their all-black schools instead of transferring them to less crowded schools with white students.

School integration is one of the most serious questions facing school boards today. If the student body does not have an equal balance between Negro and white students, the school board might be suspected of illegal discrimination. If the school board does not permit transfers, the suspicion arises that transfers are refused to prevent integration. If the school board does permit transfers, it may be criticized by dissident neighborhoods who object to receiving students from other schools.

Track system — right or wrong?

The Superintendent of Schools of Washington, D.C., resigned in 1967 over a clash between what he believed was correct educational policy and what the Federal District Court ruled was required by laws protecting minority rights. The school system had what it called a track system. Based on ability shown in the classroom and on tests, students were classified into two academic groups. The top group got a college prep course. The lower group took a vocational course. A group of parents attacked the track system as discriminatory. The District Court ruled that it was illegal to put students into two categories in this manner, and the superintendent resigned.

The best way to get this problem into focus is to review our statement of purpose: "The purpose of schools is to educate children."

The first answer to the complex question of racial integration in the schools is this: examine it as an educational question, not only as a social, legal, constitutional or political problem. Students learn more than just the academic subjects in school. They learn about people and attitudes as well. Colleges recognize this when they try to attract students from distant states and foreign nations.

Similarly, grade school, junior high school and high school students can learn more about their world in an integrated school. Justice and decency demand rapid recognition of the rights of Negroes. To prepare children better for the world they live in, schools must help them overcome mistaken beliefs that white and black children have about each other. One way to let them learn how to live together is to teach them in integrated classes.

Overcrowded and partly-filled

In Chicago there are overcrowded high schools in Negro districts and partly filled classrooms in all-white schools. Viewed as an educational problem, this is wrong. The school board handles public money and has a duty to use this money to educate all children who attend public schools. Chicago has a superintendent who is determined to overcome this problem.

Remember that integration is not the only problem that a school board has. It is only one of a variety of serious difficulties facing all people interested in public school education today. Some people become so excited about integration that they forget that the purpose of the schools is to educate children.

Earlier in the chapter we mentioned the Washington, D.C., school decision on the track system. This is an example of the distortion that can happen if parents act as though integration is the only problem the schools have.

The school policy that the objecting parents attacked was the track system that placed students into categories. The theory was that too many Negro students were on the lower track. The question of what kind of education would be best for the benefit of those students apparently was considered irrelevant. Every educator knows that there are students who shouldn't go to college. This isn't because of their race or color, but because their performance, interest in academic subjects, willingness to work, and encouragement from parents may be lacking.

Are all the choices wrong?

If integration is viewed in a light other than how to provide the best education, you find yourself going in circles. If Negro students are sent to an all-Negro school in their neighborhood, they are discriminated against because of color. If white students are bussed from the school nearest their homes to a distant, predominantly Negro school, discriminating against the white students is alleged by some. A policy of free transfer at the student's request can result in segregation, and so can a policy of permitting no transfers. The school official seems faced with a series of potentially wrong choices.

But look at the problem as an educational problem only. You represent all the students. Provide them with the best possible education. Your students will have an edge in today's competitive world if you impart knowledge impartially and fairly without race consciousness. You know you can't do this in segregated schools.

The Supreme Court ruling prohibiting prayer in the public schools is on the books and must be obeyed. It's not difficult to avoid a prayer, but it can be a little difficult to decide what constitutes religious education.

The Supreme Court has not outlawed the study of the bible in literature courses. Students must be familiar with the bible to understand English literature. This can be done without making the study a course in religion. Religious interpretation of the bible should be left to the parents and churches.

Many different kinds of troubles facing schools have pushed educational theory into the background. I repeat that schools are meant to educate children. It's time to bring educational theory back into focus.

However, this is not a book on educational theory. I won't tell you how to teach Johnny to read, nor how to understand the new math. I do know that as a school official, citizen, or parent interested in good schools, you must be concerned with the educational methods your school uses. What does the school do to arouse the students' interest? What competitions, like science fairs and similar projects, are there? Are the primary students really learning to read?

During a recent controversy over the phonics method of teaching reading, I asked a veteran grade school teacher how she taught. "A good teacher uses every method. If the school policy is to use just one, she bootlegs the rest."

Forming of teachers' unions

More and more teachers are forming unions. School boards that never expected to face the problem now must learn how to negotiate contracts and get along with unions. Much can be learned from the experiences of other school boards that have faced the same problems.

Teachers are demanding higher salaries, smaller classes, better facilities, more fringe benefits, a voice in school administration, the right to select courses, and many other concessions. One big union made over 200 demands in one city — despite the fact that its teachers were among the highest paid in the nation. Like members of other unions, teachers will strike to enforce their demands. When teachers strike, the children lose.

It is not easy to meet the teachers' demands and avoid a strike. When you raise salaries, add teachers, or build new classrooms, you need new sources of revenue. Most communities have heavy tax loads now, so you need tact, persuasion and a sense of urgency to sell a new tax increase.

What I have said elsewhere in this book about using experts

for effective local government applies to negotiations with unions. No businessman with a budget as large as a school board's budget would send an amateur to face a professional union negotiator. Your school board attorney or a local businessman can help you by recommending an experienced negotiator. The negotiator will not make your decisions: that isn't his job. He will see to it that your position is presented and protected as strongly as possible.

You can look ahead by getting a candidate for the school board who understands unions. Give this some serious consideration at your next election.

You need a word of warning. If teachers are being approached by union organizers in your district, do not try to discourage them. School boards have found that opposition does not prevent the unions from organizing, but it does create resentment and distrust. The union will be more militant and hard to get along with when it is organized. Besides, some tactics used against unions are illegal. You cannot threaten to dismiss anyone for union organizing or union activity of any kind.

Can you legally deal with unions?

Some officials in some states contend that they cannot legally deal with a union. A governor of California raised this point during efforts to unionize college faculties. This puts local school board officials in a bad position, because if they do not deal with the union they might have a strike. If local law prohibits dealings with unions by school boards, it must sooner or later be changed. The legislature or court decisions will change it. The trend toward teacher unionization is too strong now to be opposed.

I have not forgotten that most teachers are as devoted as anyone else to education for children. Some are more devoted than most people: in one large community they even passed up a raise to win concessions for their students. On the other hand, teachers — like all professional people — want higher incomes. We have seen how successful they have been in getting higher pay during the last decade.

All this is leading to a shift in the balance of power. Parents' groups that have been able to run school districts according to their own best judgment, through their school boards, now are discovering to their dismay that unions are formidable competitors for control.

Even parent-teacher associations are, in some cities, breaking up into warring factions. This puts additional pressure on school boards. Boards must be alert, flexible and aware of their ultimate job: to educate the children.

Convincing argument

A few years ago alert officials averted a threatened teachers' strike in Oklahoma. School board officials pointed out that state law required a minimum number of school days per year. Any time lost in a strike would have to be made up by delaying the next summer vacation. This was a convincing argument.

There are actually four groups that sometimes fight over control of the schools: parents, teachers, administrators and the school board. In Tulsa, teachers and administrators argued over the control of the Tulsa Education Association. Washington, D.C., parents disputed with the administrators for control of a school. For several years the former superintendent in Chicago fought openly with his school board, claiming that any detailed decision they made interfered with his domain as administrator.

Often the problem of integration in the public schools is in part behind the warfare that goes on. There are usually complex local problems that build up before there is an open clash.

While there is no easy solution to intergroup controversy, it's helpful to place the problem in perspective. And that is to never forget the needs of the children. Each of the fighters will claim that what he wants is "what's best for the children," but you can test him by his actions. Any individual or group that works to protect its assumed authority even at the expense of orderly schooling for the children is not helping to educate them. This should answer parents' strikes as well as teachers' strikes.

As in any other kind of struggle, the best defense is a good offense. A school board that has a vigorous program of providing new services has an excellent chance of earning the respect of the public.

Adult education programs

Elmhurst, Illinois, has had an adult education program for some years. Many other school districts cooperate with the state university to provide courses in elementary education. The purpose is to attract qualified men and women into public school teaching. Ordinarily the school board can charge tuition for adult education; thus, this program can be set up without increasing taxes.

Junior colleges require tax money, and securing it may be easier than you think. There will be a continuing huge demand for college education in the coming years. Figure 34 shows the rise in the number of young people just under college age. In a few years this surge of graduates will enter colleges. The chart cannot show the fact that college work is becoming more necessary to meet competition in the job market. Machines and computers do the routine work that high school graduates once did.

Many youths will be disappointed in their efforts to enter college. A junior college will help them in two ways. First, they will be able to get at least a year or two of college to prepare them for the competition in the job market. Second, the late starters will have a chance, by producing a high record in junior college, to transfer to a senior college later.

If your district seems too small to have a junior college, don't give up. Cooperation is the key. Have the school board's attorney investigate if you can legally form a junior college jointly with other local school districts.

A junior college may help solve the dropout problem. A good student who has no money to go away to a university may be encouraged to enter a local junior college.

Project Head Start is a program you can run on a shoestring, if necessary. While the work is not easy, some volunteer part-time help can be recruited. Check with nearby communities to learn how they managed. Contact the United States Department of Health, Education and Welfare for advice and aid. You can't insure exact equality of opportunity, but you can offer hope where there has been despair.

Be willing to join, and work with, local, state and national associations of school board officials. These groups will keep you up-to-date on how other boards are meeting problems that are like the ones you have or will have soon.

Remember, the school board is ultimately responsible for the schools. It is responsible to the public that elects the board, or elects the people who appoint the board. The board must set the policy that will, hopefully, make a success of the school system.

10

Welfare and social work

WELFARE AND SOCIAL WORK directly or indirectly affect just about every local official's job. If welfare workers are successful in getting people off the relief rolls, everyone in the city benefits. Business prospers from an increased work force and taxpayers pay less because of a cut in the cost of relief. All benefit from the easing of unrest caused by unemployment and aimlessness. Everyone's civic pride rises.

Local officials should acquaint themselves with the many imaginative ideas that have worked. Although there are all kinds of federal aid programs, local officials administer them. There are also local funds, primarily real estate taxes, for welfare aid. There are state agencies, but most of the duties are performed by county or township welfare workers.

Often welfare workers face a feeling of hopelessness. A woman writer from England was interviewing girls in families that received aid. The visitor was pleased to find a girl who said her life's ambition was to "draw" — until the writer discovered that the girl meant to draw aid to dependent families.

Self-defeating cycle

There is a self-defeating cycle that welfare workers must fight. People who get welfare can get into the habit of thinking that since they can't do anything else, they might as well give up and stay where they are.

Sadly enough, one aspect of the law seems designed to keep people on relief. If a relief recipient earns a little money by working part time, without notifying authorities that aid payments be stopped, he can be arrested for fraud. Faced with the choice of living on aid alone or being guilty of fraud, it's easy for him to decide to live without working.

The local welfare worker can help by instilling a positive attitude. There always will be a few people who, whatever happens, won't work. Still, most people would rather have the satisfaction of earning their own living. The welfare worker must encourage the recipient to stand on his own feet.

Cook County, Illinois, the county that includes the city of Chicago and dozens of suburban towns, has large numbers of people on welfare rolls. Cook County experimented with assigning welfare recipients to work in the public works department. When recipients found that they could do useful work, they gained hope and ambition.

It's important to note the difference between welfare programs, such as aid to dependent families, and unemployment compensation. Unemployment compensation is not welfare: it's similar to insurance, and it pays compensation to a person who loses his job, in accordance with premiums paid by the employer. It is based on former earnings, not on need.

The welfare worker who is trying to make his recipients independent should know what Oklahoma City officials did recently. After giving away food through the Federal Surplus Food program, they stopped.

They found that certain recipients wouldn't look for work as long as the free food held out, but they would seek employment when they got hungry. This is a type of drastic change that can do harm, however. There are people who desperately need help, and cutting off all aid increases suffering.

Welfare work can benefit from cooperation with other agencies. In Cook County, all child adoptions must be investigated by a social agency. The job is too big for the County Welfare Department. Licensed charitable child welfare societies arrange adoptions by finding a home for a child and a child for the home. The court takes the agency's report as evidence of whether or not the home is fit for the child.

Private agencies do not handle all adoption investigations, however. The Cook County Welfare Department has a court service bureau that makes an investigation when the court assigns the job to do it. The social worker at the agency will not only check whether the proposed home is fit, but also interviews the mother who is giving up the child to determine if she is sincere and has no reservations.

Adoption, foster homes and delinquency

In adoption, the child becomes a son or daughter with the same rights as a person born into the family. A child in a foster home, on the other hand, is not legally a son or daughter, and can be moved from home to home. While many foster home placements are done by private adoption or child welfare agencies, there is one field that local public welfare or probation workers conduct: homes for delinquent or dependent children.

Most children who break the law and get into trouble do so because of their environment. Probation officers sometimes help such a child by placing him in a foster home. All public officials should know that foster home placement can be an effective way of rehabilitating delinquent children without confining them in an institution.

Caseworkers' duties

There are several steps that a caseworker must go through to provide a foster home. First, he investigates the people who want to be foster parents. Their reputation in the neighborhood is checked. The caseworker comes to the house to see if the housekeeping is at least average. He checks what kind of sleeping arrangements the foster child will have. If the home is adequate, and the foster parents are sincere and able to provide a good environment for children, he approves the home. In states that require foster homes to be licensed, the caseworker will process the application and secure the license.

Next, the caseworker must find the best-suited child for the home. The workers don't try to match people for foster homes as closely as for adopting homes, but they place a white child in a white home and a Negro child in a Negro home.

Finally, the caseworker arranges for cost payments to the foster parents. In the Chicago area, foster parents receive about $60.00 a month. Many local agencies also provide medical care, and reimburse the foster parents for clothes. Foster parents are not permitted to make a profit.

Did you know that in Europe there are social workers who place old people in foster homes? The social worker takes an application from an elderly person who needs companionship, but who doesn't require nursing care. He finds a home where an older person is welcome and where there is something useful for him to do.

The time may come when a local official in our country will try this idea. It won't be easy, but it can be, and is being done. There are several benefits: the old person has companionship, the family receives whatever light help he can give, like babysitting, and his financial contribution to the family can be less than his cost of maintaining a rented room.

This could be an unorthodox but effective substitute for institutional care for the elderly who have no money. The county welfare or other local welfare departments could pay a monthly amount for expenses to foster homes. It should be easy to figure if paying a foster home to take an old person would pay for itself. First, determine the cost per person for care in the county home. A simple way to do this is to take the total budget of the county home and divide by the number of people it can accommodate. This total budget must include building maintenance, the cost of building bond issues, and current operating costs. It might cost less to divert money into foster care rather than into a new building.

Obviously, not all the aged in the institutions are able to live in foster homes. Some require special nursing care. Some are too crochety to live harmoniously in a family. The caseworker must determine who is eligible. He must be careful in his selection of foster homes for the elderly, just as he must be in finding homes for children.

Special needs of the elderly

There are many ideas under consideration to benefit the aged. Chapter 3, "Recreation and the Challenge of Leisure," explains how local government can meet certain needs of senior citizens. The federal government recognized the special needs of the elderly for community services in the Older Americans Act, which provides for local governments to establish community facilities. Federal aid comes from the Administration on Aging, Department of Health, Education and Welfare, and is channelled through the state public welfare department.

It's difficult for a public official to determine if social workers are doing a competent job. Here are suggestions to help you understand what welfare people do:

The caseworker handles individual problems. These include

aid to dependent families, help with delinquent children, placement of children in foster or adopting homes, and anything else that has to do with strictly individual needs. Marriage counselling is an example. A few divorce courts have caseworkers who try to save marriages.

Qualified caseworkers

A fully qualified, professional caseworker has a master's degree. He earned it partly by academic study and partly by work in the field. He also needs perserverence; otherwise he might give up, for example, when a client shows a lack of interest in self-improvement. He requires imagination and a sincere desire to encourage people to get along without his help.

Group workers differ from caseworkers by supervising groups rather than individuals. Those who work with juvenile gangs are group workers. Persons who organize activities such as field trips may be group workers rather than recreational personnel. While they cooperate with groups, eventually they hope to achieve results for the individual.

Area workers covering an entire locality are sometimes considered to be social workers. They may wander into political activity rather than social work. Volunteer workers with no special training sometimes become confused and carry on political activity instead of social work.

In Tulsa, VISTA workers called a protest meeting to attack alleged discrimination in park facilities in Negro residential areas. The meeting didn't draw too many people, and there were no visible results. This was mainly due to the lack of experience of the VISTA workers. A more effective way to obtain additional park facilities is to approach the park board with an offer to help. Chapter 2, "The Revolution in Park Land Management," relates how anyone can help a park board determine needs. The protest meeting should be a last resort and not a substitute for hard work.

There are people in every community who are dissatisfied with the way things are, but who waste their energies or do nothing because they don't know how to proceed.

For example, in 1965, it was revealed that babies in a publicly-supported Chicago hospital were being neglected. A sincere woman said to her friends, after reading the morning paper, "That's awful. We've got to do something. Let's organize a protest march."

A protest march won't give the babies their bottles on time, but properly-channelled volunteer help will. Many hospitals have a program called Candy Stripers. It provides for volunteer girls to visit patients and relieve the nurses of routine jobs. The Red Cross Gray Ladies help at veterans' hospitals.

With some ingenuity, welfare workers should be able to divert people from protest marches to help in other, more productive areas. Besides hospital care, "clean-up week" has worked in some cities. Instead of carrying signs reading that the alleys are dirty, people should clean them. Organized groups are working to help find employment for those who want to work. If a building needs fixing, it'll be repaired sooner by offering to repair rather than by having a rent strike. Try offering volunteer clean-up labor to the landlord in return for materials and skilled labor.

Volunteer help can't replace professional welfare workers but it can aid them in getting more done. It can also provide an answer to protest marchers.

11

Where does the money

come from?

A LOCAL OFFICIAL WHO understands the fundamentals of finance can provide more services for less taxes.

In addition to levying taxes, local governments can charge for many services. There are numerous sources of federal aid, and not all is restricted with red tape. Proper planning of bond issues can save enough in financing costs to do much more for the community.

The Village of Hanover Park got along for over a year after it was formed before the first tax money started to come in. Hanover Park was incorporated so that local residents could control the development of farm land into subdivisions of homes first, and commercial land later. Under· the procedures for collecting taxes, over a year passed between the election to incorporate the village and the time the first tax money came in.

One way the newly-elected trustees of the village got along was by collecting a realistic sum for building permit fees. In a new village, a large part of the clerical cost of running the village can be attributed to expense related to building and subdivision control. Building permits were taken out so regularly that a dependable source of income resulted.

This doesn't mean that building permit fees should be set as high as you please. The fees must be reasonably related to the cost of administering the building department. The fees can be higher, though, than the mere cost of paying the building inspector's wages. Some clerical work can be figured in.

Should the city make money?

The question of how much a city can make out of any service is a controversial issue. Some water department officials contend that it's improper to earn a profit on water rates. Still, many cities regularly charge some of their clerks' salaries and other overhead costs to the water department. There are two risks that must be considered. First, too much diversion of the water funds might be illegal. Check with the city attorney. Second, if too much money is taken out of the water department, there may be insufficient reserves for depreciation of equipment, new construction, or for periodic inspections and repairs.

Almost any kind of a local government, from cities to fire protection districts, can find sources of service charges to supplement tax income.

Park districts can charge for swimming pools. Season tickets and daily admissions may be sold. Beware of charges in areas where there is poverty — don't make it impossible for people to use the pool. Your purpose is to give service, and the charges are useful only if they increase, not decrease, city services.

Chapter 6, "Mass Transportation, Railroads, Waterways and

Airports," discusses the value of an airport authority. The airport authority not only can collect rent from the airlines, restaurants and shops, but can charge a landing fee for each private or commercial plane.

Many cities make a charge for collecting garbage and refuse. You can add it to the water bill to eliminate the cost of separate billing.

Certain cities levy a permit fee for special events, requiring anyone staging a game or circus to pay a sum toward the cost of extra police work, including directing traffic.

A sewer service charge will cover the cost of providing sewer mains and sewage treatment plants. If the city offers both water and sewage treatment service, collection is fairly easy. Threaten to turn off the water if the entire bill, for water and sewer service, is not paid. If sewer service comes from a separate local government entity, such as a sanitary district, collection is more difficult. You might consider a contract between the city and the sanitary district to allow the city to make collections on the water bill — if this is permitted by your state laws.

License fees for businesses

Besides service charges, the city can charge license fees for various kinds of businesses. There is a great deal of controversy over the amount that a city can charge for a license fee. The laws vary from state to state and even from business to business. For example, in Illinois, a village can license building contractors, but not plumbing contractors. Check with the city attorney before you say publicly what your city board plans to license, and how much you plan to charge.

School districts can charge tuition under certain conditions. If your school district is to have a junior college, you may find it necessary to make a nominal charge for each hour of study. Grade and high school students from outside the district normally pay tuition. If your district takes students with special needs, such as physically-handicapped students, by agreement with other districts, the other districts should pay tuition.

Schools have shown considerable ingenuity in raising money for special projects. Admission charges for football, basketball and baseball games can help support the athletic department. If you've no sports stadium, rental with the owners of any stadium may be arranged. Doubtless you'll need to pay the stadium owner a share of the gate receipts, but even then it'll probably cost less than financing and maintaining your own city stadium.

All schools charge student fees to help pay costs of activities and equipment.

For special purposes, the PTA can have a party. Many stage a Halloween costume party to raise money with games, movies, and the sale of donated goods and foods.

No matter how many ideas you have, you probably must levy a real estate tax, too. This tax is supposed to be a percentage of the value of the privately-owned real estate in the community. Actually, it is a percentage of the assessed value, not the actual value. Some tax assessors use a fraction of the actual cash value. Others do, but don't admit it.

Tax collecting systems

The system for collecting taxes varies from state to state, and the time it takes to get the money back to the taxing bodies may be anywhere from a few months to nearly a year, depending on the location.

In most cities, the amount of the tax bill has been increasing steadily from year to year. Figure 40 shows the tax rise over a ten year period for a $15,000 home in a typical community. Taxes can't keep rising rapidly forever. Local governments must seek other sources of revenue.

Estimate how close your community is to a dangerous rise by charting the rise in tax rates over the last ten years. Be sure to

take the total rate, not just the city tax. The total tax rate
includes the city, school district, county, and any other special
taxing district rates. Use the records at the county court house
or your own records if you've lived in one place for ten years or
more. Figure 41 will help you visualize the trend.

Federal aid, while it has helped in some limited areas, isn't
the whole answer. Federal taxes can't rise forever either, even
to save local government. Federal officials in Washington have
problems visualizing local solutions to local problems. I doubt
that we'll see an end to the federal aid trend.

Chapter 12, "The Growth of Federal Aid," suggests what
federal aid is available for your projects.

Your local government's tax money and revenue from fees,
charges and licenses will buy more capital improvements, such
as new buildings or water works, or more land, if you know
how to plan bond issues properly.

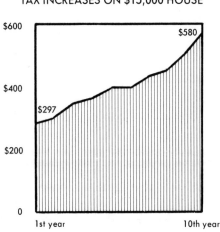

Fig. 40
TAX INCREASES ON $15,000 HOUSE

Typical tax increases in Midwestern suburbs. Rates have risen to over
$70 per $1,000 assessed evaluation in many towns in and around Cook
County, Ill.

Chapter 7 listed the three kinds of bond issues that can be used for any kind of a capital improvement: general obligation bond issues, revenue bond issues and special assessment bond issues. The right combination can get the job done for the least cost. Reducing the interest rate by one per cent on a 20-year $500,000 bond issue will save more than $50,000 cash.

Fig. 41
TAXES IN YOUR COMMUNITY OVER TEN YEARS
House with a market value of $15,000

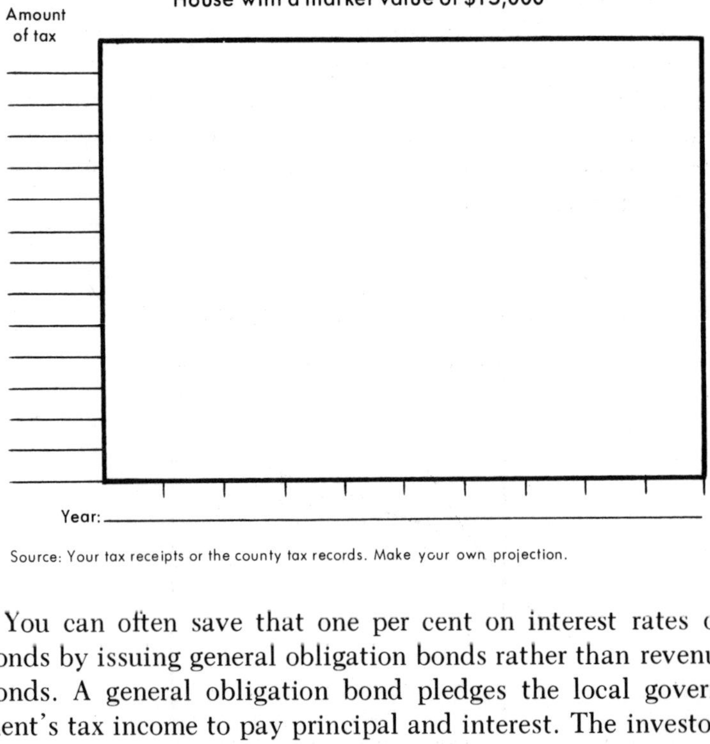

Amount of tax

Year:

Source: Your tax receipts or the county tax records. Make your own projection.

You can often save that one per cent on interest rates on bonds by issuing general obligation bonds rather than revenue bonds. A general obligation bond pledges the local government's tax income to pay principal and interest. The investors know they will be paid whether the facility makes money or not. Local governments that have power to levy taxes can sell general obligation bonds.

General obligation bonds can be used to build buildings

such as a new city hall. Chicago and Cook County worked together to erect a combined city hall and county courthouse, called the Civic Center. In this cooperative venture, the city sold bonds for the west half of the building, and the county sold bonds for the east half.

Other types of local government agencies can work together to build a dual-purpose building.

Geneva, Illinois, built a combination field house and high school building. The school board financed the classrooms. The park board paid for the field house. The high school could use the field house for a gym, during the hours when school is in session; that is, when there is the least demand from the public for the park's field house. Similarly, the park district could use the classrooms for activities after school hours.

General obligation bonds

There is a limit to the amount of general obligation bonds that a local government can issue. In many states, the limit is five per cent of the assessed value, and in some cases it is as low as two and one-half per cent of the assessed value of all property in the city or district.

Some theoriticians say that this five per cent debt limit is the reason we have so many overlapping local governments in the same area, such as a park district, a city or village, a school district, a fire protection district and a library district. Chapter 1 points out the real reasons why local governmental units are formed; that is, to put a particular problem in the hands of responsible people really interested in solving it.

I know of no local district that was formed to circumvent the five per cent debt limit. In fact, there is a way that a local government can issue bonds for more than five per cent of its assessed value, involving the proper use of revenue bonds.

The five per cent debt limit does not apply to revenue bonds. This is one of the factors that makes revenue bonds a valuable aid to municipal finance. A city can issue general obligation bonds up to the limit, and then issue revenue bonds for the balance needed. Other factors being equal, the local government will issue as many general obligation bonds as possible first. These pay a lower interest rate.

Chapter 2, "The Revolution in Park Land Management," pointed out that a park district can rely on revenue bonds to buy land for anything from airports to zoos. The same is true of any local government. Any project that will bring in revenue is a candidate for revenue bonds.

Water revenue bonds show how a revenue bond issue gets paid. The city places all its cash from water bill collections into a special account. First, it pays the cost of running the waterworks, called the operation and maintenance fund. The next portion of the income goes into the depreciation fund. After that, the amount needed for principal and interest is placed into the bond and interest fund. The rest of the cash can be assigned to various reserve accounts.

The water rates must be high enough to cover the cost of running the system and to pay the principal and interest due on the bonds.

Any other kind of a revenue bond issue is based on a similar plan. The cost of operation and maintenance comes first, then depreciation, then the bond principal and interest, and finally the reserve accounts.

Cost and income study

None of the tax money can be used to pay off the revenue bonds; therefore the cost and probable income must be studied carefully. The study that shows the anticipated costs and income over the life of the bond is called a feasibility report. For many public works projects, the city engineer or a consulting engineer hired for the purpose prepares the feasibility report.

A third kind of bond issue is the special assessment bond issue. Special assessment bonds are paid off by people who own property that benefits from the work the bonds paid for. If collections are not good enough, the bonds don't get paid. During the 1930's and 1940's, many special assessment bonds were in default.

In some states the city can guarantee payment from tax funds if special assessment collections are not good. Special assessment bonds in these states are more secure, and easier to sell. If cities in your state cannot guarantee payment of the special assessment bonds, your city will have to pay a higher interest rate for special assessment bonds than for either general obligation bonds or revenue bonds. The exact rate depends on local history and local conditions: that is, on how safe the bonds look to the investors, in view of past history and the condition of the land. It is difficult to sell special assessments now for vacant, unimproved land. Too many investors suffered losses years ago financing sidewalks and water mains in the middle of pastures.

We can see how important it is to have other sources of revenue besides taxes by examining the problem of the local public schools. Schools have very little revenue except property taxes. They don't have a water rate or a building permit fee to help with the costs. The athletic fees, football and other sports tickets pay only the costs of the athletic department.

This means that school taxes are the largest part of local taxes. Figure 42 shows the division of the real estate taxes in a community in DuPage County, Illinois. The schools take about four-fifths of the tax dollar. This doesn't mean that the schools cost four times as much as all other local governments. It means that the schools don't have much income except from taxes.

Keep this in mind when you are looking for ways of raising money: schools can't keep taxes down. Other local governments can help by looking for money from the sources of revenue outlined in this chapter.

Cities are using a new avenue of income in the last few years, the municipal sales tax. When the idea of a city sales tax first became widespread a few years ago, local merchants fought the idea because they thought a sales tax would drive shoppers away. Actual experience shows that this did not happen. In most cases people paid a state sales tax anyway, and the additional city tax was not enough to drive them out of town.

I hope you haven't surmised from this chapter that the local government's most important job is to raise taxes. The fact is, though, that people are insisting on more and more government service. The flight to the suburbs brings people who are accustomed to full city services and facilities. As population increases, services will need to be increased. Each community is faced with the question of how to pay for additional services — and it's up to you to find a way.

Fig. 42
TYPICAL PROPERTY TAX BREAKDOWN

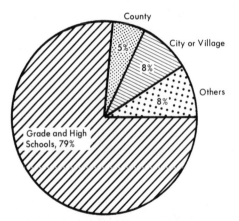

The percentages will vary greatly from one location to another. Cities have many other sources of revenue besides local real estate taxes. Therefore the city's share of local income is really greater than 8%. The 8% estimate is for real estate and property taxes only.

12

The growth of federal aid

THE SURVIVAL OF LOCAL government will depend in part on how federal aid is handled. So far, all of the legislation for federal aid to local governments has provided for a large amount of local control of the spending. There is danger that local control might gradually slip away, however.

There is even a greater possibility that federal aid could be used to favor large metropolitan governments or even regional governments at the expense of local governments. This has not yet occurred. It is something to watch for whenever a new federal aid program is proposed.

Another problem that federal aid brings is the matter of local resistance in some towns to any kind of federal activity. In 1966, the Lombard Park district held a referendum on the

Fig. 43

TYPICAL KINDS OF AID THAT THE FEDERAL
GOVERNMENT HAS GIVEN LOCAL GOVERNMENTS*

Department or Bureau	Program	Kind of Aid	Part of Cost U.S. Pays
Dept. of Agriculture	School lunch	Grant	1/4 of cost
Dept. of Commerce	Green Space Public works acceleration in areas of unemployment	Grant	1/2 to 3/4
Dept. of Commerce	Highways	Grant	From 25% for local highways connecting with interstate systems, to 90% for interstate expressways
Bureau of Census	Special census	Special service	Bureau of Census provides some personnel, but local government pays all costs
Dept. of Defense	Civil defense	Grant and supervision	Not over 1/2
U.S. Army Corps of Engineers	Create inland waterways	Grant	All costs except port facilities
U.S. Army Corps of Engineers	Survey to prevent shore and beach erosion	Grant	Cost of survey
U.S. Army Corps of Engineers	Park and recreation land at water resources development projects	Special service	U.S. has authority to lease recreational land to local government such as a park district or forest preserve district
Dept. of Health, Education and Welfare	Vocational education College buildings Student loans Educational TV Library extension services Community health services	Grant and loans	Various grants and loans
Dept. of the Interior	Water resources research Recreation facilities	Grant	Grants or matching funds up to 50%, through state officials
Dept. of the Interior	Water resources research Recreation facilities	Grant	Grants or matching funds up to 50%, through state officials

Department or Bureau	Program	Kind of Aid	Part of Cost U.S. Pays
Office of Economic Opportunity	Job Corps Community Action	Direct aid	Costs paid, but local cooperation is required
Federal Aviation Authority	Airport planning	Grant	Cost of planning
Dept. of Housing and Urban Development (HUD)	Housing and home finance agency. Public works planning	Loan	Advance must be repaid
HUD	College housing	Loan	Loan to college
HUD	Urban planning	Grant	Grants
HUD	Urban renewal	Grant	2/3
HUD	Preserving open space	Grant	Grants
HUD	Mass transportation research	Grant and loan	Grants and loans

*This chart shows sample programs only. A complete list of all federal aid programs would be a large catalog. Programs change from time to time, as does the money available. For detailed information, contact the agencies listed above.

question of issuing bonds to buy land. At the same time, the park district asked, on a separate ballot, "Shall the park district apply for federal aid for land acquisition purposes?"

The park board didn't need to call a referendum on the question of federal aid. The aid was available under the green spaces program of the Department of Agriculture without a referendum. The idea was to find out what the people of the village thought about federal aid.

The results of the election seemed easy to predict. Who would turn down "free" money? The unexpected happened. Lombard did!

Before your city can decide whether federal aid is a threat or a boon, you'll have to understand just what federal aid is. There are three kinds: First, a federal department or agency can loan money to a local government for a local purpose. Second, the United States can give an outright grant instead of a loan. Third, the federal government can provide a direct service to the local community by agreement. In this case, the local authorities might have to pay for the service, as happens when a city asks the census department to make a special census. Figure 43 shows the forms of aid available.

An example of each of the three types will show how federal aid works.

A federal loan carries with it a considerable amount of federal control. The Village of Bridgeview, a suburb of Chicago, borrowed money for its water system by selling bonds to the Housing and Home Finance Agency, a branch of the Federal Housing Authority. The procedure was for the village to call for bids on the sale of its bonds. When there were no bids that would give the interest rate specified, the village applied for and received approval of the sale of its bonds to the government.

The regulations for the way the work had to be done were very detailed. The rules even described the kind of a sign that had to be erected to tell the world that the project was made possible by federal aid. Each day the contractor had to turn in forms with multicolored copies to show the hourly rates he was paying. Every payment to the contractor by the village had to go through the proper channels. Unlike the Lombard park district, Bridgeview was satisfied with its federal aid, despite all the extra paper work that came with it.

Preparing plans

Your city must prepare plans for its public works project before it can sell bonds to finance it. There is a federal loan available for the cost of preparing plans.

The Department of Housing and Urban Development has interest-free loans for planning many kinds of public works except most public buildings. Not only sewer and water, but also school buildings, recreational facilities and roads can be planned with this money. Such a loan, or advance, is repaid when construction work is started. By that time, the city is required to have found some permanent financing, by means of a bond issue. The bond issue must be large enough to cover the repayment of the planning advance. The proposal must conform to the local plan or to a state or regional plan.

A grant is more favorable to the local government than a loan is. This includes certain programs in which the federal government pays all the cost, but many more where the federal government pays only a percentage of the total cost.

Think ahead when acquiring land

Chapter 2 emphasized the need for looking forward to acquire more land for park districts than you think you need immediately. The same advice applies to other public bodies. Inflation of land prices, the disappearance of vacant land in the community, and the increasing needs for land for various public purposes make it imperative that a municipality secure as much land as possible without delay.

The Department of Housing and Urban Development has grants for part of the expense of buying land to be used within five years. Don't be misled: this grant does not cover the cost of the land. It covers the interest on the cash that you borrow to buy the land. The advantage is that you are able to buy land when it is still vacant, before inflation has increased its cost, without paying extra interest even though you bought the land a few years early.

In many communities the cost of land approximately doubles every five years.

The grants described here are only a few samples of the many different federal grants for communities. The Department of Housing and Urban Development will send you catalogs and pamphlets on its latest programs upon request. The Office of Economic Opportunity has other plans in their catalog. Don't give up just because nothing was said here about the type of project you have in mind or because you've never heard of federal aid for whatever you plan. These programs change rapidly and availability of money flucuates.

Many local officials overlook the help that their city attorney can offer when they seek federal aid. Some think they need to find someone with special influence. Since the question of the aid that is available is first a question of federal law, the lawyer is a logical man to start with.

Local officials who use federal aid also can talk to their United States congressman or senator about the problem. Legislators have research staffs to help people find answers. Such aid can be helpful and time-saving.

Direct service aid

The third type of federal help mentioned, direct service by agreement with the federal government, can involve something that will dramatically affect the future of your town.

Fort Smith, Arkansas, is to have a waterway as a result of a United States Army Corps of Engineers project. The project will widen and deepen the Arkansas River, which flows from Fort Smith to the Mississippi. All of the work of widening, deepening and dam construction will be paid for by the United States Army Corps of Engineers. Fort Smith won't pay any of the cost of the river channel.

Fort Smith will, however, have the expense of installing harbor facilities that it needs. In this sense the federal project is not free to the community. Communities along the Arkansas River are planning facilities, holding referendums, issuing bonds and buying land for port facilities.

These plans must be made jointly between the federal and local government officials. The Army Engineers and the city officials meet and work out the details. It would be unrealistic to ignore the role of United States congressmen and senators in bringing such a project to a locality. There is never enough money for every possible project. Some fighting must be done for each area.

The Army Engineers have made economic studies to prove that the Arkansas River Project will pay for itself over a number of years, as it serves cities inland as far as Tulsa. The added business that the project will bring into the Arkansas basin will more than offset the cost of construction, spread out over a period of one hundred years.

Similarly, the St. Lawrence Seaway Project improved the existing waterway linking the Great Lakes cities, including Chicago, with the Atlantic Ocean. Some ocean-going vessels were able to use the route even before the work was done. The project deepened the channel so that deeper draft, heavily laden ships could go through. This was an improvement to every commercial city on the Great Lakes, at the expense of only the extra harbor facilities they built to handle the added business.

Lists of available aid

Any list or chart of federal aid that's available shouldn't be taken literally. There may be changes since the list was published. Congress often changes the amounts appropriated for various projects. The President can limit expenditures when inflationary threats or war costs require a cutback somewhere. The value of a list is to suggest possibilities for further study, not to provide final answers.

A lawyer recently stated, "There are federal officials sitting on huge sums of money in their offices, almost frantic because no one knows how to come in and apply for it." Actually, there's more to it than that. Many local officials don't think in terms of getting federal money. Perhaps they agree with the Lombard voters who turned down federal aid in their referendum.

There are a few lawyers who specialize in making applications for local governments for federal aid. Some grant and loan programs will set aside a sum to pay the attorney's fees. Your city attorney can tell you if he thinks this is necessary in your case.

Still, the most persistent problem connected with federal aid is the policy question of whether the city should take the aid. No one can answer this question for your community except yourself. There is no doubt that federal aid brings with it federal controls and red tape. On the other hand, it is certain that the people in your community will pay federal taxes whether they benefit from available aid or not. Their federal taxes include money that will be used for local governmental purposes. If you do not take any of that money, the local taxpayers still pay for it, as well as for local taxes for full services.

They are, in a sense, paying double taxes for local government services.

Refusal to take federal money is not an appropriate form of protest, anyway. If you oppose federal taxes for local government purposes, the place for the fight is in Congress. If you don't take the aid, someone else will.

Much of the controversy today is not over whether there should be federal aid to local officials, but over how much control the federal government should exercise. A few hopeful state governors want federal tax money to be turned over to the states and local governments with no strings attached. Others point to a few abuses and insist that more federal control is needed.

Loss of local control

Obviously, the power to hand out money will carry some control with it, no matter what local officials want. It is possible that the desire to administer the money on a metropolitan or regional basis will strengthen metropolitan or regional government at the expense of local government. What we said in Chapter 1 about the importance of strong local control of local affairs is vital here.

Local officials will have to exert constant vigilance to make sure that federal money is not used to abolish local government. This cannot be done by ignoring federal aid. It might help if local governments prove that they can handle federal aid projects on a strictly local basis, with little federal supervision.

13

How to pass a referendum

THE LOMBARD PARK district is so successful with referendums that it has lost only one in decades.

A school district a few miles from Lombard recently lost an election to increase its tax rate. A nearby city lost an election to sell bonds and collect taxes for a new water works. A village lost an election for a new city hall. All these nearby local governments have one thing in common, though: each one later won the referendum for the same improvement that it lost the first time.

The fact is that there is a right way and a wrong way to present a referendum. Getting the voters to vote "yes" is a major selling job. There are no short-cut gimmicks that guarantee approval. However, sound methods based on proof that the project is needed will generally win a favorable vote.

An elected official begins to win or lose his next referendum the minute he takes his oath of office. Even if he doesn't know it, he will need a referendum sooner or later.

The first step to win a referendum is to handle all the public's affairs with honesty and integrity. One reason the Lombard park district always comes up with a winner is that the public has confidence in the park board.

In a fast-growing community in Illinois, village officials planned a system of sewer mains to serve a part of town that has only septic tanks. As the work progressed, the village officials continued to approve large bills for more material than could possibly have been used. Citizens' protests were ignored, and the final cost was thirty per cent over the estimate.

Later, the same village board had a referendum for a general obligation bond issue to pave the streets. Many of the streets were bumpy and unattractive. Citizens were complaining about the old gravel and mud roads. It is obvious how the election for the paving bonds came out. The voters would not trust the board with the money.

The second step in passing a referendum also takes place before you have a definite plan for a referendum worked out. Whenever representatives of an organization ask for a service you cannot provide, or cannot provide fully, tell them why. If you don't have enough baseball diamonds for all the Little League teams, tell their chairman that you want more land. Get his name, address, and telephone number. Ask if you can count on him when you need help with a referendum.

Getting people to help

Your secretary or clerk can keep a file of the active people whose organizations want the next referendum to pass. When you are ready to release publicity for the referendum, call the people on the list. Usually this will be after you have a definite plan, know what you are going to build or buy, and have estimated costs not only of construction but also of financing. You have an understandable package to present.

The third step toward victory is to take your time. The village board members of a small village knew they had to add to the sewage treatment plant, because more people wanted to live in their community. In September of that year, the engineer presented the plans and cost estimate. They began to consider a date for holding the referendum for a bond issue.

At first they talked about a December election date, but the engineer pointed out that in December, people would be worrying about their Christmas bills. He suggested the election be held sooner. He convinced the board that the election should be held in October.

Rushed voters vote "No"

Anyone whose town has made the same kind of a decision knows what happened. That election did not carry. The voters did not have enough time to learn why they needed a new plant. When the voters are not convinced, the majority most likely will vote "no."

It takes several months to get the story across. Remember, you will need newspaper articles. Try to secure radio and TV coverage, too. Even if yours is a small town in a large metropolitan area, there probably are some programs that feature local civic news. Support news releases with public talks, pamphlets, meetings with civic groups and word-of-mouth advertising.

Avoid tax bill time

The fourth step to win is to avoid holding the election right after the real estate tax bills come out. Tax bills usually are higher than many taxpayers expected. People grumble for awhile when they receive the bills. It doesn't matter that you are only one of a number of local governmental organizations that share the tax money. You may get only a small percentage of the local real estate taxes. You might even have reduced your own tax rate. The voters see the entire bill, and they vote on the impression they get from it.

You might get away with breaking this rule. Once in a while a referendum for a bond issue will carry at tax bill time. If you do not need the money for a month or two, you will be better off to wait until the taxpayers have a chance to cool off. If you try to have the referendum before the tax bills come out, make sure you start several months before. Hurrying so fast that the voters can't be well informed has lost many more elections than it has won.

Fig. 44
HOW TO SHOW SCHOOL ENROLLMENT

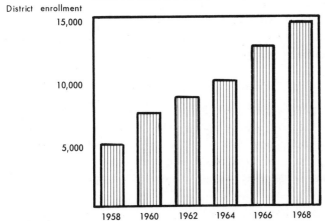

This is based on typical figures and is not taken from any one school district. For your referendum, use your own enrollment figures.

The fifth step is to distribute pamphlets that tell your story in chart or graphic form. A few pictures help, too.

Figure 44 shows how a typical, growing school district can chart its growth before a successful referendum.

Another graphic idea worked for the Tulsa library board. A picture of a young girl using the library was printed on the cover of a pamphlet urging approval of a proposed bond issue. The caption read: "A Library for Linda."

No matter what kind of local government you have, there is a way to present your story dramatically. A simple bar graph showing growth of the population of the area you serve will help. If you are working for a new library building, compare the number of books taken out the first year the old library building was used with the number of books today. Use a bar graph or a sketch of two books; a short one for the old figure and a long one for the current figure.

For a special tax to increase police department pay, you can secure figures on major crimes for the entire United States from the FBI's Washington, D.C. office at: Federal Bureau of Investigation, United States Department of Justice, Washington, D.C. 20535. You may or may not want to use the local figures, too. If the number of local crimes is increasing rapidly, it is an argument for more police.

Show voters their gain

For a bond issue for new fire engines or new fire stations, check the effect on the insurance rates. You may be able to work out a chart showing a drop in insurance rates as a result of better fire protection. Take various amounts of insurance for comparison, so that you can show the savings on $10,000, $20,000, or $30,000 in fire insurance.

One imaginative park board president used a simple plan to dramatize the low cost of his proposed bond issue to buy enough land for the next ten years. He figured that for the average home in the district, the cost of additional taxes would be about $5 per year. This is less than the cost of taking the whole family to the movies, even without popcorn. The president pointed out that the voters could use playgrounds, trees, shrubs, walks, and tennis courts (see Figure 45) as often as they wanted, for less than the cost of one night at the movies.

Fig. 45
HOW TO SERVE AN ENTIRE PARK DISTRICT WITH NEW PARKS

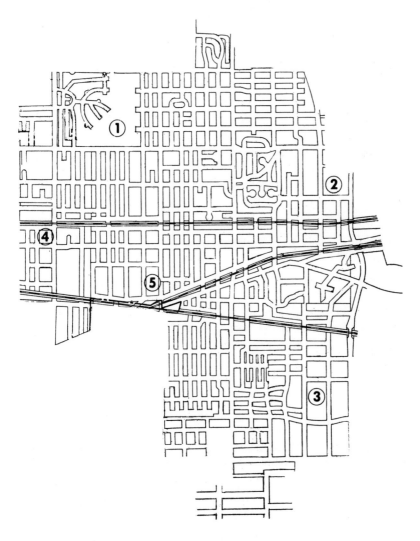

1 through 4: Proposed neighborhood park sites
5: Large community center park
Adapted from successful referendum plans

The pamphlets that you circulate will need more than a dramatic chart or graph, though. Tell the complete story, frankly and clearly. Do not emphasize the obstacles. Be positive. Remember that you are asking busy people to take their time to read the pamphlet, so make it readable and understandable.

To convince the voters, you must show them how they will benefit. Don't sell a desperate need, sell the benefit to the public. The public does not want to hear how shaky the old fire engine is. Describe how the shiny new one will protect their homes and reduce insurance rates.

Sources of literature funds

Consult your attorney for sources of funds to pay for the pamphlets. You may need to rely on contributions.

The sixth way to help pass a referendum is to have a package that will serve the entire city; that is, the entire park district, library district, or school district. For a park site, do not buy just one park site, get several around town. If you need more fire protection, and if the area is big enough to use two fire stations, put them up both at once, not one at a time. Use pamphlets to show the entire city how you are locating the improvements for the benefit of all.

You may need a referendum for a new school for just one corner of the school district, even if there is no need for new construction in the rest of the district. Lombard had this problem a few years ago. People who had ample schools near home asked, "Why should we pay for a new school we don't need?" The answer was that if the new school is not built the children in the new subdivision would have to go to the old schools. This would mean overcrowding and split shifts, with less effective schooling for everyone.

The referendum passed in all the precincts.

Of course, you could appeal to the voters' sense of fairness, and inform them that another part of the city needs help more than their part. This probably would not work. Many voters will not vote to pay higher taxes unless you can show that they benefit, too. The benefits might be indirect rather than direct. For example, a homeowner without children benefits both immediately and at long range from better public schools. Good schools will keep his property values up.

The seventh part of the plan to pass a referendum is to have lots of people help you promote the project.

You should have started making the list of possible helpers long before the referendum was ready. If you kept up the list, as suggested in the second step of this chapter, of everyone who asked for more service than you could give, you would have a good start. Have your clerk or secretary pull out the list and ask one of the elected members of your group to call the people listed and request their help.

Citizens' groups

Many public bodies have their own citizens' groups. The library should have the Friends of the Library. The school board can call on the PTA. The park district might enlist the camera club.

A committee of public-spirited citizens can help. Appoint those who have been complaining that there are not enough facilities.

The committee that you appoint can assist you in many ways. First, the members can do any of the tasks listed in this chapter. Second, they can set up a "telephone tree" for the day of the election. A telephone tree seems to work best with women. On the day of the election, each leader in the telephone tree has a list of five people to call. She gives each of these five her own list of five to call. The leader calls back later to make sure all the calls were made. That way each leader can influence thirty votes.

The committee members are also useful when it is time to pass out pamphlets. They can work to get the vote out on election day by the methods outlined later in this chapter. They are quite helpful in word-of-mouth advertising. Such a person is often active in one or more civic groups, and can boost the referendum at meetings of community leaders and interested citizens.

Many people think it is difficult to pass a referendum for more than one local body politic at the same time. Tulsa proved that this is not true. In 1965, Tulsa successfully passed a referendum for an art museum, parks, and a library system all at one time. Figure 46 shows the added tax that voters were asked to approve. Despite the headshaking, all the proposals passed. During the referendum, proponents of each part of the referendum pushed for all three parts. This multiplied the number of salesmen by three and no doubt helped get out the votes.

Fig. 46
REFERENDUM ON THREE ISSUES

Three new taxes voted at one time.		
	Art museum:	$ .28
	Parks:	2.50
	Library system:	5.06
	Total added taxes:	$7.84

Source: 1965 referendum in Tulsa. The amounts are based on taxes to be levied on a home with a market value of about $10,000.

The eighth method of passing a referendum is to have two kinds of meetings.

One is the usual public meeting. Invite members of the board who can think fast at the speaker's table. Make sure that you have enough facts to answer all questions fully. Usually it is better not to offer refreshments at this meeting. Someone is sure to ask, "Who is paying for the refreshments?"

Most public meetings work out better if they are divided into a few short talks on the needs, and an unlimited question period. It is not unfair to plant a few questions in the audience, but you probably won't have to. Public meetings where the public is invited to ask questions have a way of becoming interesting.

Sometimes the law requires a public hearing before a project can get started. Even if the law doesn't require it, a public hearing in a hall large enough for everyone who wants to come will increase your chance of winning the referendum.

The second kind of meeting is entirely different from the public hearing. It is a coffee meeting among the people who support the proposal. This may be for twenty to thirty people who are mildly interested and inclined to favor the proposal. Unlike the large public hearing, the idea is not to argue with possible opponents, but to let the people who are with you gather strength. The meeting can be in anyone's home.

The idea is to present facts, discuss the issues, and plan how to continue the next phase of the campaign. Lukewarm people can be won over this way. It is similar to what some candidates for election do when they have their helpers hold coffee meetings in their homes.

The ninth step may sound extravagant but it is very practical. Be generous when you plan the program that you will submit to the voters. Don't try to pinch pennies and come up with the lowest-cost program in local history.

Avoid short-sightedness

If you need new parks, buy more land than you think you need, in more places than you believe necessary. If you skip one part of town, you will lose votes there. The same applies to any other bond issue. If you plan a water works just for the present population, the voters will be justified in thinking you are shortsighted. Most people today know enough to beware of a fantastic bargain. If you estimate the cost too low, they will suspect you plan more a little later.

Once in a while a referendum will fail because there was organized opposition claiming the estimated cost to the improvements was too high. If you draw such opposition, demand that your opponents tell you what part of the proposal they would cut out. In Villa Park, voters turned down a water works referendum because of organized and vocal opposition.

Fortunately, the village president had managed to draw out his opponents to the point where they specified just what part of the equipment they thought was surplus. The village put up the same proposal, with the challenged surplus part left out, at a slightly lower cost. Those opposed were now stuck with their earlier position, and could not change their story to the voters. The referendum passed the second time. Better some water than no water!

If Villa Park had started with a meager program instead of a generous one, there could have been opposition anyway, but there would have been nothing to pare away after the referendum failed.

Rapid population growth in urban areas

A program that looks generous will look tight in a few years, anyway. We have seen rapid growth in the population in urban areas in the United States since 1920. If the present trends continue, any plan that you make today will be inadequate in a few years unless it is farsighted and generous.

The tenth point actually explains the purpose of most of the other points. Get the "yes" votes out.

It makes no difference how many people you convince that you are right. It only makes a difference how many people you get to vote "yes".

In one village, there was an election to approve a badly-needed bond issue for a water well. There were seven election officials in one precinct. These seven did not cast their own votes in the election. When all the votes were counted, the "yes" votes fell short by seven votes.

Not every case is this bad, but local elections are won or lost by the stay-at-home vote. It is not necessary to put up with a large stay-at-home vote. If too many of your supporters stay home, you will lose that election — and it will have happened needlessly.

Figure 47 shows the range, from 10 per cent to 100 per cent, depending on the effort to get out the vote. The 100 per cent turnout is not an impossible dream: like the four minute mile in track, it takes work.

Fig. 47

PERCENTAGE OF ELIGIBLE VOTERS ACTUALLY VOTING

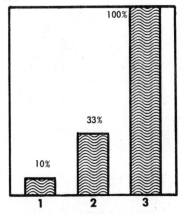

1: An election to incorporate a fire protection district
2: A typical local referendum
3: Referendum held in Buffalo Grove, Ill.

The telephone tree described earlier in this chapter is one way to make sure people get out to vote. This can be combined with the baby-sitter car ride plan. When a woman calls a voter, she asks if the voter needs a ride and someone to watch the children. If a person won't vote even with a ride and free baby-sitter, go on to the next voter. You can't twist arms to make people vote.

The eleventh method is used regularly by skilled professional politicians. You can turn pro to win your referendum. Arrange to have poll watchers at each polling place. Your attorney can make sure each poll watcher has the right kind of credentials to be able to stay.

Fig. 48

Prompt and effective service is necessary especially when the fire department is called. Such service, too, wins "yes" votes when the next referendum is called.

Provide the watcher with a copy of the list of voters in the precinct. If you can, arrange before the election to get a printed copy if the registration officials have one.

This poll watcher is not there primarily to watch for anything wrong. He is there to keep track of who has voted.

When a voter comes into the polling place, he gives his name to the clerk who checks the registration list. The poll watcher that you sent will check off the names. He does not leave unless his alternate is there to keep track while he is away. The alternate also has credentials that you arranged ahead of time.

About three or four hours before the polls close, the watcher leaves his alternate in charge, and he takes his list of people who have not yet voted. Here is where the call with an offer of a baby-sitter and a car ride can get out votes that otherwise would be lost.

If the question is important enough to put to a referendum, it is important enough to work for. If you don't have enough workers, and you lose, there will be many shocked people saying, "I thought it was so important it would pass anyway. If I knew it was going to lose by such a close vote I surely would have voted yesterday."

You might not need the twelfth step if the first eleven went right.

Don't give up the cause!

The twelfth step is: don't give up if you lose. A western community put up a million dollar bond issue for a new library building and lost. An eastern community had a $600,000 water bond issue that was turned down by the voters. A northern community had a bond issue for increased school taxes. Each of these issues ran into organized opposition and failed to pass at the polls.

These communities have one thing in common, though. Each tried again and won.

The library plan was expanded to cover branch libraries for

all parts of the area instead of just the downtown. The water bond issue was reduced in cost slightly by eliminating the part that could most safely be deferred. The school district solved its problem by cutting services to compensate for its low income and increasing costs. After a short time, the parents were willing to get out and work for a higher tax rate.

There is no one formula for passing a referendum that failed the first time. If your referendum fails, you must make a diagnosis of what went wrong. Do not put the same loser up again. You might need only a slight change of plans and technique to win, but obviously you need a change.

The school board in Bartlesville, Oklahoma, couldn't get voter approval on bonds to repair school buildings. The proposed bond issue included an item for a new swimming pool at one high school. Complaints about the swimming pool convinced the school board that it should try the bond issue in two parts at the same time, one for school repairs and one for swimming pools at both high schools.

The building repair bond issue passed, the swimming proposition lost. The question was not that the pools were or were not needed, but rather that the swimming pool issue was preventing the badly-needed school repairs. The pool issue can always be brought up again, when public opinion is more favorable.

REFERENDUM CHECK LIST

1. Handle public affairs honestly throughout your term in office.
2. When you must turn down a request for service, explain why.
3. Allow plenty of time to inform the public, at least several months.
4. Avoid tax-bill time.
5. Use pamphlets with charts and pictures.

6. Offer a package for the entire city, not just one part of it.
7. Have many people helping to sell the idea. Use a telephone tree.
8. Use public meetings: large gatherings and small coffee groups.
9. Have a generous program, not a niggardly one.
10. Get the "YES" vote out. Offer rides and baby-sitters.
11. Use the pros' method. Keep track of who has and who hasn't voted. Call those who have not.
12. If you lose, try again, with some revisions. Don't put the same loser up again.

14

Planning is dreaming

AT A RECENT ZONING hearing in Tulsa, the chairman of the plan commission asked a representative of the state mental health service, "Do you find you have more patients in cities that have a plan commission?"

If the plan commission is not blamed for mental health problems, it is probably the only thing it doesn't get blamed for.

Cities often spend a great deal of money, time and effort on planning without knowing just what planning is. You can hire expert planners. You can use thousands of dollars of tax money and receive federal aid for planning all kinds of projects from urban renewal to better sewers. You are chasing your tail, though, if you do not know what you are trying to do.

196

Planning does not mean taking a set formula and applying it to the city to determine what the plan should say. Planning is dreaming. It is the same thing that an ambitious person does when he puts his feet on the desk for a few minutes to think about where he wants to be in a few years. What is the ideal growth pattern for your home town? Do you need more apartments or more single family homes? Is there enough industry, or do you need to start a crash program to attract it? Is it primarily a city of homes with men travelling every day to work in another city? Do you want it to stay that way? In which direction will the city grow?

Only after you have answers to these questions can you be specific about zoning regulations, major streets, water plants, sewage treatment, mass transportation and the other details that make up the bulky package called the city plan.

Far-reaching planning decisions

A comparison of two villages in Illinois illustrates how far-reaching a decision on planning can be. A few years ago, Addison began a serious campaign to become an industrial village. A large area with a railroad track through it was annexed and zoned for industrial uses. When more streets were needed, the village officials called a public hearing and told the industrialists that they could have the streets with a special assessment. Interested citizens and village officials formed an industrial commission. With the help of railroad officials, industry was attracted.

This trend had a way of reinforcing itself. The people who owned vacant land near existing industries got industrial prices for their land. The local village and school taxes were lower, because industry had a higher assessed value. The low tax rate resulting from the presence of industry attracted more industry.

At the same time, Lombard elected to be primarily a residential village. Land that was annexed, more often than not, was zoned for residential purposes. This gave Lombard a reputation of being a good place to find a home, so more residents moved in. Now Lombard is working on attracting industry to balance its tax base, but the commitment is already made. It is a residential city. If you live in Lombard, you may have to drive to Addison to work.

Each of these villages could have gone in either direction at first. Thousands of people viewed hundreds of acres during the time Addison was attracting industry and Lombard was becoming residential. The areas were large enough to make their own environment. Figure 49 shows the increase in assessed value of each village during part of the rapid-growth period. After the village started in one direction, though, it became easier to keep it moving on the same course.

Interestingly, Lombard recently began a program of annexing land to be developed for industry.

Whether you plan for it or not, your town or city is taking a direction right now. You must decide which way. This is a policy decision, and no expert can make it for you.

How do you make a policy decision? One way is to do nothing. Let the events happen by accident, and then have planners decide what to do about it.

Deciding on course of planning

If you intend to plan in the full sense of the word, you will decide what course you will pursue. Start by talking to residents, property owners and businessmen. You may find that businessmen have one idea, and residents who work in another city have entirely different points of view.

Here is where many city officials err. Often if they call a public hearing, they do so after a plan has been prepared. The decisions have been made. The planner is committed to a certain kind of growth pattern. He has put his ideas in writing. His reaction to any new idea will be to view it as an attack on his plan; and he will fight to defend it.

Fig. 49
GROWTH IN ASSESSED VALUE OF TWO NEIGHBORING TOWNS

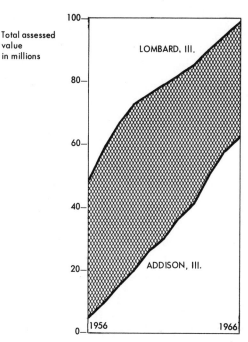

While Lombard, emphasizing residential growth, approximately doubled in assessed value, Addison, which encouraged industrial growth, went from $5,000,000 to $62,000,000 in assessed value.

The first public hearing should be held before any plan is made, about the time the planner is first hired. This is not the kind of public hearing that the law requires; rather, it is an opportunity to find out what people want.

While the decision about the sort of future desired is an individual one for each city, there are some principles to consider. First, the city is not an isolated piece of real estate all alone on a planet. It is a part of a county, of a state, and of the country. If it is not yet part of a metropolitan area, it may be sooner or later, probably while your plan is still in effect.

You must plan your city as a part of America. A city that is located along the Arkansas waterway must decide what effect the barge traffic on the waterway will have. A city that is growing must anticipate that demands for homes and decentralized industry will increase.

In an expanding suburban area, how much business will be needed to serve new residents? How many homes and apartments will be required? Do you want more industry, or more office space to encourage commuters to find work closer to home? Do you want to induce big city business to decentralize by moving to your town?

Working out the details

After you know what you want your part of the country to be like in the future, you can start to work out the details. To do this, start with a study of what you already have. Use a printed map of the city, showing details down to lots and blocks. In some parts of the country, the county has a department that can furnish such a map. In other areas, private map companies have maps. Ask for an atlas or plat showing the city. You may have to assemble several maps to cover the entire area. Tape them together so that you can picture the whole project at once. If you have access to aerial photographs, use them also.

Put in as much detail as you can. Outline the commercial, industrial, apartment and residential areas. Wherever there is vacant land, show how close the nearest sewer and water lines are located.

A professional city planner will make the same kind of start, but perhaps with even more exacting detail. If you have a professional planner working for you, ask if he will let you look at his working maps early in the proceedings.

Chapter 2, "Park Land Management," mentioned a few ways to predict population trends. You can use United States census figures to see how rapid the growth has been in the past. Contact the utility companies to learn what they plan for the future. Look at the city as a part of the total nation to evaluate how your area can move population and business your way.

If you compare the predicted population figures for your city with the actual population figures, you'll probably find that the city grew faster than anyone thought it would. In fact, many towns and cities have grown twice as fast as predicted. Eventually they catch up with their sewage capacity and must float a bond issue to add to a plant that was supposed to be adequate for years to come.

This growth can come from factors outside your town. If your town is a suburb with many people commuting daily to a large metropolitan center, growth of business in the center will bring you more residents. These added residents will create demands within your town for more stores and service industries. In turn, new stores and service industries will result in more population.

Industrial and commercial growth

Another kind of growth can come from steady industrial and commercial progress within your city. Unless you have an unusual situation, this will mean that more people will come to work in the new industries. At the same time, others will move in to run the shops and service industries for the growing population. For every four new employees, a conservative estimate is that you will need an additional employee in a service industry or retail outlet.

There are ways to predict the amount of new industry that you are likely to attract.

Fort Smith will have waterway transportation soon. The United States Army Corps of Engineers, widening and deepening the channel of the Arkansas River and building dams, will make the river navigable. Fort Smith can predict an influx of any industry that will benefit from low cost bulk transportation.

A town near a large metropolitan area can capitalize on the trend toward decentralization. Check on the kinds of industries that are moving out of the central city. Watch which major stores are moving to suburban shopping centers. What kinds of small or medium sized new businesses are starting to serve the decentralizing industry? What existing local firms will grow as a result of the changes going on?

To attract good industries, you'll have to provide what they want. No industry has to move to your city. There is competition between cities and villages for industries.

For example, how effective is your law enforcement? An industry choosing between several possible sites wants a safe place for its transferred people to live. No one wants to build a plant in a community that is unstable.

Do you have enough water to serve new industry? What plans are being made to expand the water works when you outgrow it?

Do your officials exact a bribe for approval of building permits or business licenses? See Chapter 18, "Do You Have What It Takes?" to learn how cities have successfully coped with deep-seated bribery problems.

Correcting plans

If your local government falls short, either correct it or plan on less new industry than would otherwise be expected. If your local government is exceptionally good, prepare the plan map with the idea that there may be more industry than you would otherwise expect.

These are the things that the official planners' statistics cannot measure with precision. The policy-making local officials must use their judgment.

When the map is ready and the population and business trends are noted, you will be able to start work on the most controversial part of local government: zoning.

A zoning ordinance is a regulation on the use of land. If you have never read one, secure a copy of your city's zoning ordinance from the city hall or library. You'll find that it has two main parts: the zoning map and the zoning regulations.

Do not rely solely on a zoning map. A copy can be out-of-date a month after it is made. Look at the official map at the city hall. It will be up-to-date with all the latest changes.

Figure 50 is a part of a typical zoning map. Notice that this map uses a code number to indicate what zoning district each area is in. Most zoning ordinances designate their zoning districts by letters and numbers like this.

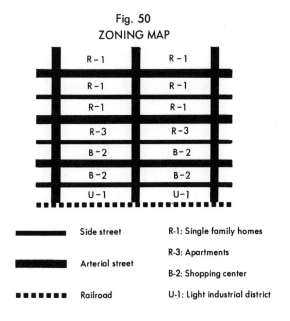

Fig. 50
ZONING MAP

	Side street	R-1: Single family homes
	Arterial street	R-3: Apartments
		B-2: Shopping center
	Railroad	U-1: Light industrial district

The second part of the zoning ordinance, the regulations, tell the property owner what he can do in any district. Most ordinances now have detailed provisions listing what can be done. The details of what is permitted in each of the districts vary from one city or village to another.

Most cities have more than one single-family residence

district. The difference between the kinds of districts is usually the minimum size of the lots. There may be more than one category of apartment districts, with more apartments per acre permitted in some than in others. There may be a neighborhood business district and a general business district for shopping centers and all types of businesses.

Usually there is more than one kind of manufacturing zone. Some cities call their districts light manufacturing and heavy manufacturing districts, but these terms are over-simplifications. Look at the ordinance and see exactly what a property owner can do in either district.

The larger cities have many different districts, to cover the many varied neighborhood problems that they have or expect to have. Tulsa has 18, others range from 5 to over 25.

Zoning factors to consider

Many elected local officials and professional planners don't realize that there are two factors that must always be weighed in deciding how to zone districts. The first factor is the public interest. What particular zoning regulation will do the most to improve or protect the neighborhood? The more knowledgeable officials ask themselves the second question, too: what special problems does the zoning create for the property owner?

In a village near Chicago, an area of land was restricted to five-acre residences. That is, the property could be used only for single-family homes on five-acre tracts. The property owner challenged the ordinance in court, and called the same planner who recommended the five-acre zoning as a witness. The planner said that he did not think the land could be developed as five-acre tracts, but he wanted to zone it that way to keep it from being developed until someone came along with a better idea.

The court ruled that the ordinance was invalid. The village had no right to prevent the land from being used for anything at all. The public interest has to be balanced against private property rights. Where the harm to the property owner is great, the court will hold the zoning invalid.

Not all zoning cases are so clear-cut. Often it is a matter of balancing possible public interest against the harm to the property owner.

There are two factors that you can consider to decide if you're treating the property owner fairly. First, what is the nature of the surrounding land? Is it a stable residential district? Is it a neighborhood that is starting to run down? Is there a trend from single-family uses to apartments or business-es nearby?

Second, has the lot created peculiar problems? Is it a long, narrow lot? Does it require great quantities of expensive fill to make it usable? What is next door? It might be impractical to use the lot for single-family purposes.

Zoning ordinances often are challenged in court. Because of the amounts of money involved, such a case often is appealed to the state appellate or supreme court. For example, in a case in Illinois, the evidence showed that a property owner's lot was practically unusable under the zoning ordinance, because it was limited to a single-family home and because there are too many businesses in the neighborhood for anyone to be interested in building a home there. On the other hand, an oil company was ready to pay $60,000 for the lot if the company could build a filling station.

It was worth $60,000 to the owner to have the zoning ordinance held invalid. He was only too willing to pay attorneys' fees to fight the case all the way.

This is not to discourage public officials to zone land for single-family uses. Whatever you do, someone will challenge the zoning ordinance. Remember, though, that a zoning ordinance must be reasonable. Any zoning can be challenged in court. The less reasonable it is, the more likely it is to be opposed.

City officials must ask for a public hearing before they can change the zoning of property. If the entire zoning ordinance is being revised, there must be a hearing or series of hearings on the proposed new ordinance and map. If only one lot or a few lots are involved in a requested change, there probably will be one hearing.

Chapter 15, "How to Conduct a Public Meeting," will discuss how to give everyone a chance to be heard, while you keep order courteously. Because the legal requirements for the kind of evidence and exhibits used vary from one state to the next, consult the city attorney regarding the procedure you will need.

Public hearings on zoning

Most state laws require that a notice be published in a newspaper before a public hearing on a zoning change. A few cities have added more notice requirements to help inform the public. Chicago tried mailing notices to people near the proposed change. Tulsa posts a sign on the lot to be rezoned, telling what the proposed new zoning is, and where and when the hearing will be.

Zoning, like many other parts of city planning, is not an exact science. All the public officials can do is try to be fair to the public and to the individual property owners involved.

After you've worked out a rough idea of the proposed zoning ordinance, the rest of the city plan can begin to take shape. Major streets will move between concentrations of business and industry. Water demands will depend on the proposed use by the various parts of the city. Sewers and storm water drainage problems can be anticipated.

Don't stick too slavishly to the zoning ordinance. Things can happen that will make the present ordinance look strange in ten years. Many cities have an official plan map that is separate from the zoning map. The plan map doesn't show the zoning that practical considerations require now. It shows the dream of the future — five, ten or twenty years away.

Planning is one field where copying someone else's ideas isn't cheating. Start by questioning officials of nearby cities. You will be amazed at how many problems you have in common. See what others have done to their plans. People and places aren't too different.

You'll still find it necessary to choose the ideas that meet your particular needs and to change them to fit your situation precisely. You'll have many more aids to planning, though, if you start with as many ideas as possible.

When you have done some dreaming, you'll be ready to tell your official planner what direction you think the city should go. Remember, the planner is only an employee of the city. The plan commission recommends, and the elected officials approve, the plan. The policy-making officials, not the planner, have the duty to guide the city's future.

15

How to conduct a meeting

AT A PUBLIC MEETING called to discuss a new pavement, the chairman got into a heated discussion with a property owner — in the Bohemian tongue. At a meeting in another city, the chairman gave a taxpayer's attorney the floor, and then continually interrupted him. In another part of the county, the mayor listened to citizens for an hour on a problem of zoning, and then announced that the city fathers had reached a decision before the meeting.

These are not farfetched examples. They are symptoms of a widespread lack of understanding about public meetings. Elected officials acquire a reputation for being high-handed by failure to understand how to handle a meeting. Some have shortened their careers through inability to conduct a meeting.

Actually there are three distinct kinds of public meetings: (1) where the public debates and votes; (2) where the public neither debates nor votes; and (3) where the public debates but does not vote.

Handling controversial subjects

The first type is a meeting where all the citizens present have a legal right to take part both in the debate and in the voting. Parts of New England have a town meeting where this happens. Illinois still has township meetings once a year where every voter can be heard, but very few people in the state know about it. Usually one or two hundred people decide the tax rate, budget and other vital matters for thousands in the township.

At this kind of a town meeting, the chairman has the job of making sure everyone who wants to say something has a chance to be heard. He can keep order by making certain that everyone will be heard once. He lets each person finish everything he has to say, and then goes on to the next. He does not return to someone who has already spoken until everyone else has had a chance to talk.

Usually the chairman will know ahead of time if something controversial is coming up at a town meeting. He can request that each side appoint a principal spokesman to discuss the main part of the argument. This idea can't be used to cut off anyone else from being heard, but it will save some time.

Take up the questions one at a time. Don't be too strict because the arguments or statements stray off the subject once in a while, but try to steer everyone to the question at hand. Some experienced chairmen never interrupt a speaker, no matter how far off course he might be. After a speaker who wanders finally stops, they will request that the speakers stick to the subject.

This doesn't mean that the responsible officials should go into the meeting unprepared and let it drift wherever it may.

The elected officials of the township, or whatever district is holding the town meeting, need definite written proposals, and they must have sponsors ready to present each proposal and move for its adoption. The chairman of the meeting must, however, be willing to permit free debate on each proposal.

After the proposal is debated, the chairman calls for a vote. The method of taking the vote depends not just on parliamentary procedure rules, but also on local applicable laws. Consult the attorney who advises the township for advice on the right way to take the vote and record it for the minutes. You may need a show of hands, a voice vote or a written ballot. The town meeting is truly a rare kind of public meeting.

Public meetings vs. town meetings

Most public meetings are like the second kind: The law does not give the public any right to participate in the debate or the voting.

The law requires city council meetings to be open to the public. The law does not ordinarily require the council to permit anyone except the members of the council to speak at regular council meetings. The public can be present, but no one can speak unless the council permits it.

Most local officials permit some limited debate by the public anyway. Setting a practical policy for this type of meeting has led to many arguments among people vitally interested in good local government. The village board in Hanover Park lets anyone in the audience stand up and ask to be recognized.

Some cities permit no discussion from the audience, and require that any discussion be taken up with individual aldermen or with committees meeting between the council meetings. For a while, Villa Park used the system of having a written agenda, with the phrase at the bottom: "I desire to be heard on agenda item No. — ." Any resident who wanted to talk at the meeting would arrive early and fill in the number on a copy of the agenda, sign it and hand it to the clerk.

There is no one right way to handle this type of meeting, where the public has a right to be present, and there is no legal requirement to let people talk. In general, the officials who let people talk freely, without any formality, seem to make the best impression. Many people go to a meeting without any prior knowledge of how to be heard. If they are shushed they'll go away angry, and if they are heard, they'll feel they had a good hearing.

Obviously, the elected officials can't help having some preconceived ideas before they start the meeting. They won't always be swayed by oratory from the public. In fact, even a comparatively large group of people at a meeting might represent a minority view of the whole city. There are some who won't bend at all from their ideas, no matter what comes out at the meeting. There usually are one or two, though, who sincerely want to know what the public thinks.

Public hearings

The third form of a public meeting is a public hearing. A public hearing is an opportunity for anyone who is interested in a question to appear and ask questions, make statements, or offer evidence. At this meeting the public takes an active part in the discussion, but does not share in the voting.

A typical public hearing is a zoning hearing. At a hearing to rezone a piece of land, the owner of the property will usually make his presentation first. Depending upon the local custom and the ideas of the attorney representing the property owner, the presentation may be very informal or very formal. In some states, legal requirements have led attorneys for property owners to present their case like a case in court, with formal questions and answers, exhibits and expert testimony. Usually the chairman doesn't have to become involved in complicated questions of evidence.

There should be a procedure to mark exhibits that are offered by anyone. All exhibits can be marked consecutively: Exhibit

1, 2, and so on. Another way some boards like to identify the exhibit is as "Proponent's Exhibit 1," "Objectors' Exhibit 1," and so on. Exhibits at a zoning hearing might be photographs, maps or petitions.

Usually the objectors to a rezoning will be quite informal in the way they present their case. If they have an attorney, the latter will organize the opposition by lining up the speakers in order. He will present the objectors' exhibits.

Working with large groups

Often the objectors have a tendency to start talking two at a time or to become boisterous in their arguments. A sense of humor can help the chairman keep the meeting in perspective. Where there is a large crowd, it helps to have the chairman make a statement at the start of the hearing. He might say:

"I see we have a lot of people here tonight. We're always glad to have people interested in what's going on in our town. Everyone who wants to be heard will be heard. I've noticed that the most persuasive statements are those that are calm and well-reasoned, so try to keep your conversation calm and reasonable. We always let the man who has asked for a zoning change to present his case first. After he finishes, we'll hear from any objectors who want to be heard. Then the proponent will have a chance for a rebuttal if he wants it."

At a recent zoning hearing in Tulsa, someone asked if a corner lot should be rezoned to permit offices. A woman who owned a home nearby rose and spoke in favor of the change. Another neighbor got up and said that the first speaker planned to sell her home. The first woman then stood again and not only denied that, but brought up other instances where the second speaker accused her of planning to sell. Finally the chairman said, good-naturedly, "We want to hear about the zoning of the property in question. You people are welcome to continue your argument outside in the hall."

Unless there is a local rule of law to change it, the officials holding the hearing don't have to make their decision as soon as the hearing ends. They can announce that they will make their decision later. The decision can be at a meeting open to the public, but not necessarily at a public hearing where anyone can talk. That is, a plan commission might hold a public hearing on a zoning question, and then discuss the question at a later meeting, where there would be no comments from the audience. The vote on the question would come at this time.

A few public bodies hold a public hearing, and then arrive at a decision at a closed session. This may be illegal in states that require all meetings to be public. It isn't wise in any case. The public will have more sympathy for what the officials are doing if there are no closed-door sessions.

The three bad examples I gave at the start of this chapter all show a misunderstanding of the purpose of a meeting of a public body. These events took place at public hearings. In each case, the chairman of the meeting failed to understand that the purpose of the meeting was two-fold: to inform the public what the public officials propose, and to inform the elected officials what the public wants. Getting carried away with arguments, trying to silence a speaker, and ignoring the ideas that come out at a hearing are all in conflict with these purposes. The public hearings accomplished nothing, and the city officials made some enemies.

Parliamentary law

I purposely avoided parliamentary law up to now. A knowledge of parliamentary law is beneficial, if you remember that it is supposed to improve democracy, not frustrate it. Use it with this purpose in mind.

Parliamentary law is mostly a matter of knowing what motions take precedence, which motions are debatable, and how to take a vote.

Figure 51 shows the most common parliamentary motions.

By using it, you can tell at a glance if a motion is in order, and what debate is in order. I'll give you an example of an actual meeting in a prosperous city in the Midwest, where the city council used most of the parliamentary moves on just one simple matter.

Fig. 51

PRINCIPAL PARLIAMENTARY MOTIONS

While these motions are on the floor:	You can still move:	You can always move:
1. Original motion:	4. To refer to committee	7. To adjourn
2. Motion to amend	5. To table	
3. Motion to amend the amendment	6. To close debate	

Fig. 52

PARLIAMENTARY STEPS THAT ARE NOT MOTIONS

Act	Purpose	Action Chairman Must Take
Point of Order	Call the Chairman's attention to a mistake of parliamentary procedure.	Chairman rules on the point, by saying the point is well taken, or the point is not well taken. He may then proceed in accordance with his ruling.
Point of Personal Privilege	Call the Chairman's attention to a right of the person making the point.	Chairman rules as in the case of a point of order.
Appeal to the Floor	Appeal the Chairman's ruling on a point of order or a point of personal privilege to the voting members of the body holding the meeting.	Chairman must take a vote on the appeal. A majority vote can overrule the Chairman.

1. An alderman moved that the city attorney be instructed to prepare an ordinance establishing legal holidays for city employees on Labor Day, Veterans Day, Thanksgiving, Christmas, New Year's Day, Memorial Day, and July Fourth. This motion was seconded. There was some debate at this point.

2. Another alderman moved to amend the motion to add Washington's Birthday. This was seconded. There was more debate.

3. A third alderman moved to amend the amendment to add Washington's Birthday and Lincoln's Birthday to the original motion. This was seconded.

At this point everything was in order, according to the rules of parliamentary procedure. There could be no more amendments, because parliamentary law stops at an amendment to an amendment.

4. About this time, the chairman of the finance committee said, "This is a finance committee problem, because it involves paid holidays. I move the entire matter be referred to the finance committee." When the mayor asked, "Is there a second to the motion?" no one spoke. The mayor announced, "The motion to refer to committee failed for want of a second."

5. An alderman who wanted to save some time for matters that were important to him moved to table the matter. The motion was seconded. No debate is permitted on a motion to table, although it was attempted. The mayor announced, "A motion to table is not debatable. The clerk will call the roll." The motion didn't receive enough votes to pass.

6. Another alderman said, "I move the previous question." That is a quaint way of saying, "I move that debate be closed and that a vote be taken on the previous question." The motion was seconded at once. This is not debatable, and a vote must be taken on it immediately. It requires a two-thirds vote to pass. The motion passed.

Instead of saying, "I move that debate be closed, etc.," some people say, "Mr. Chairman, I call for the question," or simply,

"Question." This doesn't mean anything, because it isn't a motion. It's simply a mistake.

Since the motion to close debate passed, the mayor called for a vote. Where there is a motion, a motion to amend the motion, and a motion to amend the amendment, you take a vote on the amendment to the amendment first. The mayor did this, and the motion to amend the amendment didn't pass.

Next came the vote on the motion to amend. It didn't pass, either.

Finally, the mayor asked the clerk to call the roll on the original motion, to direct the city attorney to prepare the ordinance on paid holidays for city employees. The original motion passed.

Motion to adjourn

In theory, there could be a motion to adjourn at any time. In practice, you will seldom hear a motion to adjourn before all the old and new business is finished, unless someone is irritated.

A little later at the same council meeting where all the motions and amendments were made, the mayor ruled an alderman's motion out of order. The alderman shouted angrily at the mayor and waved his finger at him. The mayor smiled and went on to the next item on the agenda.

These examples are not exaggerated. While some public bodies are able to get their business done without extensive parliamentary steps, others appear to generate all kinds of parliamentary excitement. There is no relationship between the complexity of the meetings and the amount of actual results. It is a matter of habit or tradition in some cities.

The alderman who was stymied when the mayor ruled him out of order could have fought back. Figure 52 shows parliamentary steps that are not motions but that attack procedural problems.

He should have immediately told the mayor that he had a

point of order. This would take precedence over any other matter, and the mayor would have to recognize him and let him state his point. The alderman should then have stated that his motion was in order, and told the reason why it was in order in about one sentence.

The mayor could give in and rule the motion in order, after all. He would then proceed to ask for a second on the motion.

Appealing a parliamentary decision

If the mayor still ruled that the motion was out of order, all is not lost. The alderman could tell the mayor that he was appealing the decision to the entire city council. The mayor would have to take a vote on the appeal, and the majority of the city council could overrule the mayor.

Some authorities state that there is no debate permitted on a point of order or on an appeal on a point of order. This kind of a rule is impractical to enforce. A little debate will slip in. Don't take all day with the point, though.

The man acting as chairman, president or mayor is not the only one who needs to know a little about parliamentary procedure.

In a prosperous and growing village in Illinois, the village board was considering passage of a new code of ordinances. The book to be passed had over 100 printed pages.

One of the members of the board did not want the code passed until it had had more study. He began a filibuster by reading the code, starting at page one. A member of the audience went out for coffee to keep the trustee's voice oiled. By the time the coffee came, the trustee had been silenced.

The solution was a motion to close debate. (The United States Senate is the only parliamentary body I know that permits unlimited debate). The motion to close can be made at any time. The chairman can recognize a member on a motion to close debate even though someone else has the floor. The motion was made, seconded and carried, without debate.

This is in keeping with the purpose of parliamentary procedure, to provide an orderly way for a group to get its business done. Letting one person block the proceedings by a filibuster is not orderly. Some handbooks on parliamentary law state you cannot interrupt a speaker with a motion to close debate. If you take this literally, one man could obstruct a meeting indefinitely. Most experienced chairmen won't let one man monopolize the meeting; they will permit an interruption for a motion to close debate.

The question of how to take a vote on a question causes problems. There are differences between the rules of parliamentary law as described in most handbooks for clubs, and the rules governing most local governments.

Under rules of parliamentary law, in general a majority of the members of the group make up a quorum, and if over half of the members are present, business can be done. Parliamentary practice then dictates that a majority of the quorum — that is, a majority of the members present — can pass a motion. This means that if there are ten members, but six are present and only four vote for a motion, the motion passes, even though only four out of the ten members voted "yes".

This rule doesn't work for most city councils, city commissions, village boards, or governing bodies of other local government units, though.

For example, a mayor and ten aldermen make up the city council. A majority of these eleven, or six members, is a quorum. Even if only six members are present, it still takes six votes to bind the city council. A majority of the council, not a majority of those present, is needed.

The same principle applies to most governing bodies. A city council, village board, park board or library board charged with spending public money ordinarily will pass measures only by a vote of a majority of the members, not a majority of the members who happen to be present.

There are special situations that call for a vote of more than a majority of the governing body. In some states, certain kinds of annexations of territory take a two-thirds vote. Many zoning laws require a three-fourths vote to pass a change in zoning over the formal protest of property owners adjacent to the land to be rezoned. This is a matter of local law that your attorney can check for you.

Some advisory bodies act by a vote of a majority of the quorum (that is, a majority of those present) instead of a majority of the total membership. It would be unwise to count on this kind of a local practice without asking the attorney for the board whether that is valid.

Voting in case of a tie

Under parliamentary law the chairman votes only in case of a tie. Under local government law, the president or mayor votes in case of a tie and also in those cases where more than a majority is required to pass the measure, and the measure does not get enough votes without the mayor's vote.

This won't solve all your voting problems, though. What about our example of the ten aldermen with only six present? If five vote for a motion and one against it, there is no tie. State law may permit the mayor to vote here as in the case of a tie. Check with the city attorney for a ruling.

In commission-form cities, the mayor votes on every measure. Some manager-form cities have a council or commission similar to the commission-form, and in these cities, the mayor votes on every motion.

I hope this brief survey of parliamentary and local government procedures has been sufficient to warn you not to count on your knowledge of parliamentary procedure alone.

Whether you've handled many meetings or few, talk to your city attorney and find out what you should be doing for your local government meetings.

Even the way of taking a vote is not what you might expect from parliamentary law. At the town meeting type of meeting, you get the votes of everyone there. A show of hands or a standing vote is much safer than a voice vote. It's difficult to hear the number of "ayes" and "nays" clearly in a large meeting. If local law requires written votes at a meeting, you'll need to appoint clerks to take the votes and count them.

For meetings other than town meetings, that is, meetings where only the elected officials vote, it is usually simpler to take a roll call vote. The city records will stand up much better in a court case if the minutes show the roll call vote on every motion. Have the clerk show not only how many voted "yes" or "no," but who voted "yes" and who voted "no." Taking a roll call vote in each case will eliminate arguments later.

Did you hear an argument about what a motion was, after it passed? A Chicago suburb devised an effective system to reduce such trouble to a minimum. First, all motions presented must be in writing. A motion that was not prepared before the meeting can be written out longhand and offered. Second, the city clerk and her deputy clerk attend the meetings and write everything that happens on the motions and on any amendments to the motions. This keeps the city's records clear even through some very lively discussions; and that city has lively discussions!

There is no one right way to conduct a meeting. There is one right attitude, though. The person in charge is not a dictator. He is employed, and paid, by the taxpayers at the meeting. If you are a public servant conducting a meeting, be courteous to your bosses in the audience. They will forgive you for almost any mistake except high-handedness.

16

Business regulation

is important

THE MAYOR OF A VILLAGE on the shore of a picturesque lake received an indignant letter from the president of a small manufacturing company. It read:

Dear Mr. Mayor:
Last Sunday our company held a picnic in the picnic grove in your village. After swimming in the lake, eighteen of our employees contracted skin infections. Frankly, I am shocked at your lax health standards.

This is an example to illustrate the purpose of business regulation: protecting the public and the reputation of the town. It's obvious that anyone in that company who became ill, and others who hear about it, will go elsewhere in the future, should they seek a business location, a place to spend leisure time (and money), or a community to live in. The future cost of this unpleasant incident is impossible to measure.

Three forms of public protection

It is easier to understand local government regulations if we know what their purposes are. There are three forms of protection: The first and broadest has to do with public health, such as the problem of the sick picnickers.

Next, a number of regulations are concerned with protection from fire or explosion, and with public safety in general. Finally, there is a trend toward regulations to protect civil rights, such as open housing.

A city's power to regulate businesses is not unlimited; some businesses cannot be directly regulated or licensed locally. The city attorney must read the statutes and court decisions to learn what can be licensed. If the business has anything to do with food, or drink, though, the chances are that the city has the power to license and regulate it. In some states, the city's and the county's jurisdictions overlap in matters of public health.

It is evident how much responsibility the local government in your city has for food and drink alone. Walk through the nearest business district and check every restaurant, grocery, hamburger stand, ice cream store, tavern, delicatessen, pizza palace, Chinese restaurant, Mexican cafe, popcorn store, drug store counter and other places that sell food or drink. There are also cola and sandwich dispensing machines in gas stations, laundromats, pool parlors and bowling centers. You will be surprised to learn how many places in the business district sell food.

The local government must not only pass regulations but also inspect every establishment to insure enforcement. The public relies on the fact that a restaurant open for business is proof that it meets the health standards of the community. The city must be able to justify that reliance.

Fortunately, a local government official can get certain help in food regulation. Cooperation with other local governments is useful. DuPage County, Illinois, makes its health inspectors available to city and village health departments in the county if their health ordinances meet the county's minimum standards. If a small village can't afford to hire a trained inspector, it can use the services of a qualified man, at little cost. Villages also receive advice from county health officers on what regulations are needed. This is an example of how local government can solve its problems locally without forming a regional or metropolitan governmental agency.

An expert who is called a sanitarian is employed by some communities. He is a specialist in keeping places clean, in garbage removal, sanitary food storage, and the like. For example, the sanitarian in Palatine, Illinois, a few years ago pointed out that when a grocery has frozen meat that has thawed, the meat must be marked, "Do Not Refreeze." A second freezing of the raw meat is unhealthful.

Many smaller cities rely on a local physician for advice on public health. Others have someone in town with some experience and training in the health field. It's practical to use as much local talent as possible.

Handling public health problems

Local government is obviously better able to handle public health problems than state or federal agencies. Local officers know who is careless in sanitary matters and who is not. No state or federal official would have been available to bear the brunt of local indignation in a case such as the mass illness described earlier.

For years, federal and state officials have discussed air pollution. Meanwhile, alert local governments have been doing something about this menace. Brooklyn had an air pollution ordinance in 1895. During the last 30 years, many small municipalities have passed air pollution ordinances. These once were called smoke-abatement ordinances.

Several elements are regulated in air pollution ordinances. First, the darkness or denseness of the smoke is limited. Second, the amount of fly-ash that can be emitted is held to a minimum. Third, harmful gases are prohibited. Smoke can be limited by controlling combustion, that is, having enough air and a hot enough fire. Proper combustion with adequate oxygen can limit dangerous gases.

Water pollution

Water pollution control is as important as air pollution control. Local government itself often controls sewage disposal plants, but even so there must be regulations on industries using the sewers. A simple thing like a large bakery washing sugar and other food wastes down the drain can overload a sewage treatment plant.

A midwestern town learned how to keep a large bakery from flushing excessive bakery waste into the sewers. For several months after the bakery opened, it disposed of too much flour, sugar and other food products through the drain. Efforts were made to induce the bakery to stop, but the management protested that it was doing everything possible. Spillage and wastage that could have been hauled away with garbage obviously was flushed down the drain, perhaps by workers who hosed down when they should have swept. Tests showed that the amount of food products was much higher than the sewage treatment plant could take.

At first, the town threatened fines if the nuisance continued. This didn't work too well. The bakery insisted that it was unreasonable to expect it to be perfect. Then the town tried another approach: a graduated scale of sewage treatment service charges, based on the tests of the sewage coming from the plant. The fees were set up by ordinance; the more the concentration of food products, the higher the charge. Over a certain point, the charge went up sharply. The first day after the new system went into effect, the concentrations went down, and they stayed below the danger level consistently.

The town needed the help of a qualified engineer to figure out the graduated charge, and an attorney to write an ordinance. The results show how a special-purpose business regulation can be made effective by judicious use of service charges. In this case, the charges were directly related to the cost of solving the problem, and they gave the business a valid incentive for correcting it.

Another simple kind of business regulation will ensure that no storm water flows into the sanitary sewer system. Storm water will overload it.

You can require extra grease traps at auto service stations to keep stray grease out of the system.

So important is the local control of rats that the Supreme Court has ruled that a rat inspector can enter rental property without a warrant. Rat control is particularly needed because rats can spread many dangerous diseases. The reputation of the city government will suffer if the city officials are not vigorous in rat control. Effective methods of control include not only expert exterminators, but also making sure all garbage cans are securely covered and no food is left around for rats. Rat control will not work if it is left entirely up to individual owners; one man can't keep rats off his business property if the next man doesn't. Constant inspection by local officials is the answer.

Safety regulations

Public safety regulations are the second type of business regulation. These include fire safety, building safety, control of shows and picnics where there may be large crowds, regulating the use of public streets and sidewalks for business, and prevention of fraud.

Fire safety covers much more than the regulation of buildings. The operation of gasoline stations can be controlled. Smoking can be prohibited in and around gas stations. A manufacturer whose operations create inflammable fumes can be required to have a safe ventilating system. Some cities and towns have prohibited smoking in department stores. You'll need regulations. The details will depend on the kinds of businesses the city has.

Most communities have detailed regulations for auto service stations, primarily for fire safety reasons. Usually they will require underground gasoline storage tanks. They will require vents to dissipate gas fumes outside the buildings. Often a minimum distance is specified between station and school. The building must be fireproof.

Building safety covers not only fire protection but also protection from other kinds of dangers, such as collapse or overcrowding. There are three ways for local government to control buildings:

Building codes and permits

First, before a building contractor starts work, he must get a permit. This assures the city that the plans comply with the city's building code. From time to time during the work, the builder must ask for inspections of the various parts of the construction. Thus, the inspectors can determine if the project meets city standards.

Second, in some states a municipality can license building contractors of all kinds. This means that if a contractor habitually violates the building law, his license can be revoked. Licensing is an effective method to keep the builders ethical.

Third, existing buildings used for business can be regulated. Some years ago Chicago decided to require safety doors on elevators in all warehouses and factories. Some building owners objected, claiming that this was an illegal ex post facto law, because it applied to buildings that were already up and in use, and not only to new buildings. The Illinois Supreme Court held that the city could require safety gates on elevators, even in old buildings, as a safety regulation. The city ordinance gave the building owners time to convert their buildings; thus, it was reasonable.

There are two kinds of difficulty that city officials encounter with building regulations. First, the problem of honesty among the city inspectors. Sometimes building inspectors will take bribes to approve bad construction, or for not reporting violations in existing buildings. To discover if your inspectors are honest, inquire among builders in your town. They know who is honest. A dishonest inspector is worse than useless, as he defeats the purpose of building safety regulations.

The second kind of mistake in building regulation is failure to realize that all regulations must be spelled out in an ordinance. Many well-meaning building inspectors have standards under their hats that they insist on enforcing, with no ordinance to back them up. This is illegal, and it is unfair to builders, architects and owners. One should be able to read the building code for all necessary information to learn if a proposed building method is permitted.

Performance code for building permits

It isn't necessary that a building code include every possible type of construction. Modern city officials are using a performance code. Such a code does not state how thick the wood or metal must be for a particular part of a building. Rather, it specifies how much weight a structure must hold, how much wind pressure it must bear, what vapor barrier and fire resistance qualities must be in the walls, and so on.

This allows for new kinds of construction, using new materials and methods, and keeps the building code from becoming obsolete too soon.

Any business that attracts large crowds creates problems for local government. For instance, a football stadium, a carnival or a drive-in movie will snarl traffic, unless the city does something about it. One popular measure is to require a permit fee for each event, and to make the fee high enough to cover the cost of hiring special policemen to help direct traffic.

Civil rights also are a local regulation problem. But the federal government took over this authority because state and local governments did not move fast enough. There is still an opportunity for local action. While some conditions, such as equal employment opportunities, can be controlled by federal and state regulations, real estate practices are a local problem that can be handled better locally.

There are several aspects to the problem of open occupancy relating to real estate. One is refusal to rent. Another is a homeowner refusing to sell. A third involves the real estate broker who refuses to show a house to a black in an all-white neighborhood.

The problem of brokers refusing to show a house because of race can be met with local ordinances. Many cities have already passed such ordinances; that is, in states where cities can regulate and license real estate brokers. The ordinance provides a fine and possible loss of license for refusal to show property to a prospect on account of race or color. Enforcement of an open-occupancy ordinance is difficult. Still, it will be easier to determine whether the broker obeyed or violated such an ordinance than to decide if a property owner refused to sell.

The federal government is not deeply involved in civil rights because it is especially well equipped to enforce such laws, but out of necessity. Actually, guaranteeing civil rights is a local problem. The federal government has moved in because local bodies lagged. This is no time to decide whether we want change; we will get it in any case. The question is whether local government can rise to meet the challenge of change.

17

Keeping efficient employees

MANY VOTERS NEVER attended a meeting of the park board, library board, school board or city council. Some follow the major local issues vaguely, if at all. Fortunately, the majority relate sound government with reliable public servants.

If a park worker is courteous and helpful, people will say, "We have a good park system. They treat you right."

To have good government you must have good employees. There are ways of getting dependable employees, using them effectively and keeping them.

The first step in recruiting effectively is to make it clear that jobs in your city are permanent. Don't tolerate the political custom of firing half the city hall staff every time there is an election, or when the "ins" lose.

A few years ago, I went to a clerk's office in a large city. It took three times as long as it should have to get what I needed. The man who was helping me said, "I wish it didn't take so long to get things done here. The trouble is we get all these political appointees who can't do anything. They just get in the way."

I have heard this complaint repeated in many places. You can make a test in your own city to locate possible inefficiency. If you enter an office and three of every four employees are staring at a newspaper, standing around the fountain, talking, or otherwise are not busy, you have an excess of political appointees. On the other hand, if only one man in the office handles everything, your local government may be paying money for inefficiency, which is costly, too.

While these cases are not typical of local government, they aren't fictitious, either. Travel a bit and compare what you have with what some communities within 50 miles have. When you see the calibre of clerical help that the most efficient, politics-free local governments have, you will be dissatisfied with anything less. If you locate a personnel staff that is particularly good, investigate what is done to keep employees out of politics.

A civil service program is helpful, but it's not the complete answer. Civil service ordinarily provides for oral and written tests to decide who gets a job, and allows for promotion based on tests or on a combination of tests and performance. On paper, it assures that the most qualified person will get the job.

A drawback to civil service is that it's quite difficult to discharge an employee who is inefficient. The civil service board won't discharge a man unless there is specific proof that he did something wrong. If the civil service does fire a man without clear proof against him, he may induce a court to reverse the decision and order him rehired. It is difficult to prove incompetence.

This drawback, however, is outweighed by the advantage of

being able to attract qualified people by offering permanent employment. The very fact that it is not easy to oust an employee makes the job more desirable. It attracts the kind of person who will be willing to remain for a long time.

"Temporary employees"

A civil service program can be rendered almost useless if the elected officials in charge of the local government use subterfuge. Some cities have developed a "temporary appointee" classification to avoid the intent of civil service laws. This system involves hiring a large number of so-called temporary appointees instead of holding civil service examinations to find qualified people. If local law prohibits hiring temporary employees for more than thirty days, the same men and women are reappointed every thirty days, for as long as they produce in their assigned political tasks.

Although this system raises legal questions, there is a more basic problem than legality. The problem is that it becomes difficult for the department to do its work effectively. The temporary appointees will not do as well as civil service employees. I've seen public offices where half of the staff was reading the paper and loafing. The taxpayers' money is wasted if there are more workers than are needed. It is saved if well-qualified, permanent employees are the only ones in the office.

Initiate a recruiting program to make sure you can have your pick of qualified employees. Publicize civil service examinations beyond any public notice required by law. When you can, talk enthusiastically, publicly and privately, about any opportunities that you have. For certain technical positions, you may hire someone from halfway across the country; yet, there are many people at home who can do most of the local work.

Some local governments have temporary help in the summertime, because there's no other way to meet peak demands for local service. If you inaugurate a summer playground, or a sports or swimming program for boys and girls on summer vacation from school, your demand for help will rise in the summer.

Temporary help in general needs stricter supervision than permanent help. It's the summer worker who is likely to get his hand in the rotary mower. It isn't a matter of intelligence — an "A" student home from college may begin work without sufficient training and ignore safety rules. The safe course is to let experienced, permanent help run all the machines, unless you have temporary workers who have demonstrated unusual maturity, or unless you're able to provide almost constant supervision.

Causes of injuries

Even with permanent employees, injuries can be a danger unless you know why they occur. Injuries are caused either by lack of carefully planned safety rules, or by a failure to observe and enforce them. There is no local government job that cannot be done safely.

If you don't have safety rules, or if you want to find out if your safety rules are good enough, talk to an insurance inspector or advisor with experience in industrial safety. There may be one or two simple steps that could increase the safety of your work greatly. One street department in a residential village found that it was much safer to remove snow after nine P.M.; there was almost no traffic then.

To assure yourself that safety rules are being followed by your city employees, make surprise visits. Don't settle for an explanation such as, "I've been doing it this way for fifteen years and never had an accident." As a leader, it is your job to provide leadership — even if you have to get tough. As a precaution, post signs which list safety rules, and warn that anyone caught breaking them will be subject to dismissal. It's human nature that an employee may not mind risking the loss of a toe by sticking his foot under a rotary mower — but he'll think twice if such carelessness might cause him to lose his job.

You can make it easier for the officers in your city government to work if you use the chain of command. If you're an elected official, with a department head who has several employees under him, tell him how you want the department run. If you authorize a raise, let him inform the employee. This will make the department head's work go smoother, and it won't take any of the credit from you.

Most local government and business corporations make a common mistake with their award dinners and speeches for faithful employees. They wait until a man is ready to retire to honor him.

The custom of a retirement dinner is fine, but there is a better idea. Don't wait for retirement to recognize loyal employees. Why not have an award dinner for those who have been with you for many years? They'll be better employees for it. Awards for policemen accomplish a similar purpose, but in most cities nothing is done to commend other public employees.

Acknowledging efficient employees

There are many methods for recognizing men who are years from retirement. In business, the best known is the salesmen's contest, with winners getting a vacation trip for a prize. There is no equivalent in local government, but at a public meeting, perhaps once a year, you could award certificates of achievement to those who did something outstanding.

You may have a problem with dinners for public employees. Some states and local governments don't permit them. Ask your attorney if you can use public funds for an award dinner. If not, you can still issue award certificates at a public meeting.

Don't forget the pay. Pay enough to be competitive with other employers in your city. It happens too often that competent local employees are lured away to work for private firms as soon as they learn their jobs well. In many parts of the country there is competition for good workers, and you have to be ready to meet this challenge.

It's fundamental that to attract capable employees, your government must have a spotless reputation — a reputation not only for treating your employees right, but also the public. If you have bribe-takers and stupid, arrogant men on your council, your reputation will suffer. You will have trouble keeping the better men.

18

Do you have what it takes?

ONE EVENING I WAS drinking coffee with a friend who is active in a local civic group. He had attended several village board meetings in his home town of Lombard. Honest and able to understand local problems, he was interested in improving the village government.

When I suggested that he run for office, he said, "No. I don't have what it takes to be on the village board."

He's one of the many people who are victims of a superstition. There's no magic ingredient that you must be born with to hold public office. You don't have to be a genius, although common sense helps. Most local public officials are ordinary people who are willing to try to do something for the community.

Before you decide whether you are ready, you should take stock of the reasons you want to hold public office. Are you looking for influence? Prestige? Power? You could probably achieve these aims elsewhere with less effort. Are you expecting riches in the form of a high salary? This is not the usual reward for holding public office.

I once asked a friend, a successful and worldly-wise trial lawyer with much experience representing local officials, why anyone would be interested in running for public office. He said, "Well, I guess they just want to provide a little better life for their children."

This is probably as good a reason as any. Many councilmen are too old to want children, but the idea is the same: they desire a better city for all the people.

Essentials for public officials

There are three essentials for anyone who is ambitious for public office. First, he must be willing to trust his own judgment, and not turn over his job to the experts. This may not please my friends who give expert advice on engineering, legal or city management problems, but it is true. No expert can answer the basic policy questions about the kind of a city you want. No expert knows every related field that might be affected by the advice he gives. For example, the best sewage treatment plant designers can badly underestimate the rate of growth of population and industry. As a result, their plant, designed to be adequate for ten years, may need expansion in five years or even two or three.

Second, a local official must be able to use expert advice in the areas where expertise is essential to carry out his basic policies. If you decide to enact a special assessment procedure to charge the cost of a new street to property along the road, you need your lawyer's advice not only on how to do it but also on whether it is likely to be successful; that is, will you legally be able to charge enough in the assessments to pay the amount that your other expert, the engineer, estimated you will need? There are some fields where the expert, not the elected official, has the more qualified answers.

Sometimes it's difficult to tell where the expert's comparatively narrow specialty ends and the elected official's broader judgment comes in. This is especially true in dealings between a city manager and the city council, or a school superintendent and the school board.

In Chicago, a few years ago, some of the school board members and a former superintendent had heated arguments over the neighborhood school plan. There was much public criticism because the plan allegedly resulted in de facto segregation. Whenever school board members brought up specific examples of overcrowded, segregated schools, the superintendent retorted, "That's a matter of administration that I handle. You just set policy."

That superintendent (long since departed) gave a good example of an expert trying to nullify the wishes of elected officials. If a school board just "sets policy" and doesn't make sure that each action of the administrative staff follows the policy, it is ineffective. There is no policy except as reflected in individual, large and small decisions. If the elected official is prevented by his administrators from asking any questions about the day-to-day activities, he might as well not bother to set policy. Anyone can interpret policy rules to suit himself.

Avoiding bribes isn't hard

The third essential is honesty. It's about the same thing as believing in yourself. If you believe in your own judgment, you know you can be successful without having to take bribes. Taking bribes is a pitiful manifestation of an inferiority complex.

Unfortunately, many young men entering public office let themselves be fooled about bribery. Someone who has been in office for twenty years and who has done everything wrong for

as long will impress a beginner with all his "experience". A
new public official has to be alert to protect his honesty in a
situation such as this.

How to say "No"

The indirect approach is difficult to recognize, because
instinctively we want to believe the approach is not a bribe. A
man in a little community in Northern Illinois wanted a village
attorney to be lenient in prosecuting building code violations.
He told the attorney, "You know, I didn't mean to start work
without getting a permit, but I was short of time. By the way,
I've been thinking about changing attorneys. My own attorney
doesn't seem to have time for all of the work I have. If I decide
to change, would you be interested?"

You can see how clear, yet subtle, the offer was. Although
the suggestion appears to leave the question of more legal work
unsettled, there is one thing you can be sure of. If the village
attorney did betray his client's case to please the builder, the
builder would not have trusted him with his own legal work.

The opposite approach is the direct "everybody's doing it"
pep talk. Some years ago, certain experienced township
officials near Chicago were indoctrinating newly-elected officials on bribery. One of them said, "It's the American way." It
isn't. In fact, in that case it didn't work out at all. One of the
new men bugged the meeting and recorded the conversation on
tape.

In spite of the occasional exposure, naive and inexperienced
newly-elected officials continue to entrap themselves by taking
bribes. Usually the bribe-taker is not clearly and convincingly
exposed. Often, however, there is enough suspicion to wreck a
promising career, even without proof valid in court. The
public is not as easy to fool as it may seem. A former mayor of a
Chicago suburb is snubbed by people at the train station — the
supreme form of suburban rebuke.

How do you deal with a bribe offer? Don't panic and resign,

as one young village trustee did in a midwestern community. You can set a trap for the prospective briber with the aid of the local prosecutor, if you want to. Or, you can tell the briber that you don't work that way. If the briber's approach is a bit indefinite at the start, make it clear that you aren't interested.

It takes two to effect a bribe: the one who offers it and the one who takes it. Or, the one who demands it and the one who pays. Despite protests to the contrary, there is no innocent party to a bribe. It's easier than you think to say "no."

One way to encourage the calibre of public official who won't take bribes is to provide adequate pay. In many states the pay that can go to local government officers is strictly limited by law. While there are dedicated men serving free, this system also tends to encourage bribe takers. A crook can afford to take a job that pays little or nothing. He'll make it pay.

Some regional port authorities have directors who serve without pay. This means that anyone who serves must be on leave of absence, with pay, from a business firm. The dangers of and temptations to conflict of interest are obvious. It is unrealistic to expect a man to hold a full time, unpaid job from a public agency, be on a leave of absence from his firm with pay, and have undivided loyalty to the public agency.

Everyone in public office, no matter how honest, wise, and just he may be, will be accused that he lacks these virtues. Everyone is disappointed when he is unjustly criticized. However, don't be afraid of criticism. Develop a tough hide.

I once sat at a public meeting and heard a mayor, who never did anything dishonest, being accused of taking a bribe to let a gas station be built in town. I have heard a treasurer, who was conscientious about his accounts, being accused of filing a false report. A young village trustee who favored integration in his community was charged in the newspapers and in court with scheming to block integration of a part of his town. If you are falsely censured, you're in good company.

One of the jobs that an elected official has to do is to be

ready to detect unreasonable demands. For some reason, many voters think elected officials can do anything. There was a custom a few years ago in some communities to pressure builders and subdividers into paying money to the school board. Citizens who never contributed a cent to the board would demand at a meeting that the board stop the builders and subdividers from working until they made donations. The citizens would have figures to prove that the school needed the money. The builder, who perhaps had no children in the schools, was expected to pay when the parents who stood to benefit most had made no donations either.

Some village officials have let themselves be put in the position of demanding "gifts" to the school fund. The courageous answer to such a demand is, "The village has only the taxing powers that the laws give us. We can't do what you are suggesting."

There will always be problems. There will be disagreements, discouragements, and financial crises. There will also be the satisfaction that comes from knowing that you are a part of local government, helping make the community a better place, and that you are a part of local history. If you possess honesty, a capacity for hard work, horse sense, and are willing to seek advice on technical matters, you have what it takes.

Terms in common use

Access road: see frontage road.

Ad hoc municipal corporation: a local government formed to do just one job, such as a school district, park district, fire protection district or water district. These are independent of the city government in many cases.

Airport, general aviation: an airport that is not used by scheduled airlines, but by business and pleasure aircraft. See aviation, general.

Airport, international: an airport that has flights to and from points outside the United States.

Alderman: a local legislative official who is elected from only one part of a city, called a ward. All of the aldermen, and the mayor, make up the city council, the governing body of the city.

Alley: a public right-of-way, use of which is limited to deliveries and access to property adjoining it.

Appropriation: a limitation set by local action on the amount that can be spent for any one purpose during the fiscal year. Many cities have an appropriation ordinance which sets their limits both item by item and department by department.

Assessment roll: a list of property to be charged general taxes or a special assessment.

Assessment, special: see bonds.

Assessed value: the value placed on a lot, home or other real estate for tax purposes. The local real estate tax is determined by multiplying the assessed value by the tax rate.

Aviation, general: general aviation does not mean all kinds of aviation. It means privately-owned planes, planes used by corporations for their own personnel, and planes used for pleasure — but not scheduled airlines.

Board: see village board, town board, board of education.

Board of education: the governing body of a school district. Often the board of education is independent of the city government.

Bond: a paper issued by a local government to borrow money. The bond states that the local government will pay back the amount borrowed, with interest. Usually the interest is shown on coupons, which are clipped and presented for payment every six months. There are three kinds of bonds usually issued by local governments: a **general obligation bond** is a bond that is paid out of tax money and any other money that the local government has. The government must find a way to pay this bond. A **revenue bond** is payable only from the revenue of a particular improvement, such as a swimming pool or airport. The city does not have to pay the revenue bond unless there is enough revenue from the facility to cover it. A **special assessment bond** is paid only out of collections from the part of the city that benefits from an improvement, such as a street pavement. Special assessments may be used for water mains, sewer mains, sidewalks, and anything that benefits a local part of the city.

Bond paying agent: a bank or local governmental officer with the job of taking in coupons and bonds and paying the owner the amount due. Payment is made out of a special account set up for the purpose.

Bribe: any offer of cash or any valuable advantage, used to influence the way a public official does his work. See graft.

Building code: a set of regulations in a city ordinance passed by the governing body of the city, specifying requirements for all kinds of buildings. Most of the regulations in the building code are for new buildings, or for alterations of, or additions to, existing buildings. Some building code regulations are applied to existing structures as well: the owner can be notified to change the building to bring it up to the minimum requirements.

City: a municipality governed by a mayor and aldermen, or a mayor and commissioners, having general powers of local government. A city may or may not have a city manager. See municipality, village, town.

City code: a collection of all of a city's ordinances in one book.

City commission: see commission form city.

City council: see alderman.

Civic group: an organization of citizens in one part of a city or in an entire city, which gathers information on local issues and attempts to influence local government. Many civic groups are organized as not-for-profit corporations.

Civil defense unit: a branch of city, village or county government that works with state and federal officials to prepare for the results of natural disasters or enemy bombing action.

Commission form city: a city governed by a **city commission** consisting of five or six commissioners. The mayor is one of the commissioners. Each commissioner has charge of one department of the city, such as the public safety department for the police and firemen. The commissioners meet to pass ordinances and to handle other matters of importance to the entire city.

Commissioner: a member of the governing body of a commission form city.

Condemnation: a case in court whereby a local government takes land from a private owner without his consent. A jury decides how much the government must pay for the land. The power of a local government or other government to take land this way is called eminent domain.

Corporation, not-for-profit: a corporation organized by private citizens for civic, charitable or religious purposes.

Department of Defense: the division of the United States government that is in charge of dam construction, through the United States Army Corps. of Engineers.

Department of Health, Education and Welfare: the division of the United States government that most closely affects school districts.

Department of Housing and Urban Development: the division of the United States government in charge of some of the programs affecting local governments.

District: a type of local government formed to handle only one problem, such as a school district, drainage district, fire protection district, library district or airport district.

Drainage district: a local government formed to provide drainage of storm water by improving existing streams and by building ditches and sewer mains.

Election: a vote of all voters who go to the polls. An election may be a referendum on a question of public policy, or a vote to select public officials. Sometimes a referendum on a question of public policy will be held at the same time as an election of officials.

Eminent domain: the power of a local government or any government to take private property for public use: see condemnation.

Federal aid: advice, planning, loans or grants of money, or a combination of these, given by the United States government to local governments. Regulations for receiving federal aid are set by Congress.

Fire Department: a part of the city government having the duty of fighting fires and making fire prevention inspections.

Fire Protection District: an independent local government set up to do the work of a fire department, usually in a rural area where there is no city fire department.

Frontage road: a road that adjoins a limited access highway to provide additional access to adjoining land. Sometimes a frontage road is called an access road.

General election: an election that comes at regular intervals, such as the United States election for President, every four years, or the election for city officials, every two years.

General taxes: taxes paid by all owners of real estate within the boundaries of a city, county, school district or other local government.

Graft: an illegal or questionable acceptance of cash or favors from suppliers or contractors doing business with the city. See bribe.

Health, public: alludes to assistance which a city or county can offer, or regulations it can impose, to prevent disease and guard the public health. This includes, for example, regulations for food stores, restaurants, and nursing homes. It pertains to the control of sanitation and air pollution. Furnishing health services to destitute persons also comes under this heading.

Home rule: this term sometimes is used to describe the kind of local government that can set up or change its own charter by local referendum. As a general term, it means anything that encourages local control over government affairs.

Independent school district: a school district which is a separate local government, with its own boundaries and its own elected board of education. See school district.

Library board: the governing body in charge of all library services. In cities where the library is a part of the city government, the library board may be appointed rather than elected. There are some library boards that are independent of the city; their members are elected.

Library district: an independent local government, run by a library board that provides library services. Usually a library district will cover a wider area than just one city or village.

Limited access road: a freeway, expressway, superhighway or toll road. On a limited access road there usually are entrance and exit ramps every few miles.

Local government: any government that covers an area smaller than a state. This includes cities, villages, towns, school districts, counties, fire protection districts and the like. For a complete list, see Figure 1 and Figure 2 in Chapter 1.

Manager: an appointed official who is the head of all of the departments of a municipality. In cities, he is the city manager; in villages, the village manager.

Manager plan city or manager form city: a city that has adopted the form of government using a manager as the head of all departments.

Mass transportation: moving people by bus, elevated lines, subway, or train.

Mayor: the highest executive officer in a city. Sometimes the title of mayor is used for the president of a village. The mayor is a higher officer than the manager, where there are both.

Metropolitan government: a local government covering more than one city in a metropolitan area; it may cover one or more counties. This is in effect in only a few places, such as Dade County, Florida.

Municipal corporation: this is a broader term than municipality. A municipal corporation may be any kind of local government from a city to a park district.

Municipality: a city, village or incorporated town. A form of local government that has broad general powers for police, fire protection, building regulation, business regulation, street construction, waterworks and sewage treatment. It differs from an ad hoc municipal corporation, which is formed for one kind of service, such as a park district or an independent school district. See also city, village, town.

Navigable waterway: see waterway.

Ordinance: a legislative act passed by a city council, city commission, village board, or other local government governing body. An ordinance may be a business regulation, a traffic law, or a provision for a new bond issue.

Park: any publicly-owned outdoor area used for recreation or relaxation.

Park board: the governing body of a park district. Where the park district is independent, the park board is elected by the voters.

Park building: any structure in a public park, including a field house, shelter or bandstand.

Park district or independent park district: a separate local government unit, with its own governing body (park board), responsible directly to the voters. There usually are independent park districts wherever the city itself does not provide park services through a city park board.

Paying agent: see bonds.

Plan, city plan or official plan: a written prediction or proposal, with maps, adopted as a statement of city policy. The plan suggests the way the city is expected to grow and develop, through new streets, zoning changes and construction of public facilities of all kinds.

Plan commission: a body of appointed people whose duty it is to study the city plan, hold public hearings, and make recommendations to the city council for proposed changes in the city plan.

President: the highest executive officer of a village.

Recreation: any activity, organized or random, designed to provide fun, play and diversion.

Referendum: an election on a question of public policy, such as an amendment to the state constitution, an amendment to a city charter, a question of issuing bonds, or raising a school tax rate. In some cases, a referendum is advisory only, not binding, but in most cases the result of the referendum is binding on the officials; if the voters turn down a bond issue for a new city hall, there can be no bond issue.

Revenue bonds: see bonds.

Sanitarian: a trained health official who inspects public places for cleanliness, garbage disposal, food storage procedures and any possible health hazards.

Sanitary district: a municipal corporation that provides sewer services.

Sanitary land fill: a method of refuse or garbage disposal that covers all refuse daily and follows strict specifications.

School board: see board of education.

School district: an independent local government having the duty of furnishing public schools. Sometimes there are separate school districts for the grade schools and the high schools. There are usually a number of schools in a school district.

School, public: any educational institution supported by tax money. Usually this term is used to cover kindergarten through high school, but some boards of education also have junior colleges.

Sewer: an underground pipe to take storm water or waste from homes and businesses. **A sanitary sewer** is designed to take only waste from homes and businesses. **A storm sewer** is to take rain water. **A combined sewer** will take both at once. Most of the sewers being installed now are not combined sewers.

Special assessments: see bonds.

Special election: an election that does not occur at regular intervals, but is called for one or several purposes, such as to hold a referendum or to elect an official to fill a vacancy. See general election.

Street, arterial: a street that takes traffic from one part of the city to another, instead of serving just the properties along the street.

Street, curvilinear: streets laid out in curves rather than straight lines.

Streets, gridiron: streets laid out in straight lines at right angles to each other, making rectangular blocks.

Taxes: local taxes include real estate taxes, personal property taxes, intangible taxes, sales taxes and fees charged for licenses to run certain businesses. Vehicle tag charges are a local tax. Taxing powers are set by state laws. See general taxes, bonds.

Town: a municipality governed by a town president and board of trustees. It is quite similar to a village and is not to be confused with a township. See village, township.

Town board: the board of trustees governing a town.

Town meeting: in some localities, important decisions for the meeting, at which each citizen present votes, not just the elected representatives.

Township: a township is a unit of local government that does not have as broad powers as a city, village or town. A township maintains roads, has some public aid, and sometimes provides water or sewer service.

Trustee: see village trustee, town board.

Village: a municipality governed by a village president and board of trustees. Village refers to the form of government, not the size of the municipality. Villages have nearly the same powers as cities.

Village board: the governing body of a village — a village president and six village trustees.

Village trustee: a local legislative official elected from an entire village, having the same powers as an alderman in a city.

Ward: one of the divisions of a city for the election of aldermen. Some cities have two aldermen from each ward; a few have only one per ward.

Waterway: a canal, river or other channel deep enough for barges and tow boats. A navigable waterway can take vessels with a draft of nine feet, and has locks to get around all dams or obstructions.

Zoning ordinance or zoning code: a set of local laws dividing the municipality into separate zones or districts, limiting the ways real estate can be used in each district. One might be for single family homes only, another for stores, and so on.

Index

DATE DUE

DEC 1 2 '72			
	DEC 12 '72		
GAYLORD			PRINTED IN U.S.A.